THE MOLE PENTHOUSE

Also by Gary Galsworth

Yes Yes
A book of poems

Beyond the Wire
A book of poems

nothing itself
A book of poems

The Mole Penthouse

POEMS
Gary Galsworth

Thank you to the editors of the following publications
in which these poems first appeared:

Alexandria Quarterly, "Late in the Day"
Bitterzoet Magazine, "Adobe"
Main Street Rag, "Afternoon"
Pioneertown, "Is That The Secret"
Poydras Review, "A Steady Trickle" and "Cowards and Heroes"
The Opiate Magazine, "Iterations"

© 2024 Gary Galsworth
All rights reserved.

Published by
Close Hand Press, Providence, Rhode Island, USA
ISBN
979-8-218-52845-4

Book Design
Iwan Sujono
eOne Design eone.com.au

Editors
Janis Levine, Justin Millan, and Gwendolyn Galsworth

Printed in the United States of America

Cover Art Acknowledgement

The art on the front cover of this collection, "Soen Nakagawa in the Beecher Lake Lodge," was painted by Harry McCormack (oil on canvas, "50 x 50," 1974).

Harry and I sat many Zen sesshins (retreats) together in the 1970s. Our Zen community was close knit, very enthusiastic and energized about Zen practice—and full of respect and affection for Soen Nakagawa Roshi, our Japanese Zen Master.

Our inclination was to try and get "IT" from out there somewhere ... reach a distant, mysterious, and elusive goal. A goal that would solve our issues and promote our place in the order of things.

Soen tried in his firm, good-natured way to have us see that what we sought was already in our grasp, had already embraced us completely; we had only to pull back the curtain of our attachments and self-centered ambitions to realize it.

We can see the gratitude Harry felt toward his teacher in this painting. And in expressing it, he gave a gift to all of us who felt as he did.

There were over a hundred committed Zen students in our sangha (community). Harry was one of the bright lights of that extended family. As a fellow artist, I'm pleased that he got to continue his painting, his art, for much of his journey among us. After all, what is art but our personal quest to purify and clarify this experience, this journey, as Soen might say, through eternity.

I want to thank Harry's wife, Miyuki, for so graciously giving us permission to use Harry's work in this book of poems.

Also, Rula and Jim Carr, owners of The Vault Art Gallery in Jacksonville, Florida, for their generous help in this effort.

And of course, a deep bow of gratitude to Harry.

Dedication

Janis Levine
(Soshin, her Dharma name)

Janis and I were good friends. We became good friends. I first met her at a Zen retreat at Dai Bosatsu Zendo in the Catskills. She was the cook, the *Tenzo*, and I a Zen student looking for a late-night snack in the kitchen. My friend Vinnie had found a jar of cashews on his foray and recommended them.

Janis had spent some years in Japan studying Tea and sitting Zazen at Ryutaku-ji with her beloved Zen Teacher, Soen Roshi. So, an old hand at this, she promptly threw me out of the kitchen. Tenzos are known to be no nonsense (but there was an attraction). We later dated in NYC, got married, moved to Hoboken, NJ, and had a son, our Danny. He was born with a serious birth defect and, in his long recovery, we shared some of our closest times.

As happens, our marriage failed. And as happens with kids involved, our divorce was a difficult one. My plumbing shop was only a few doors down from our house—now Janis's house—so easy to stay involved with Danny. And to my great good fortune, speaking with another separated dad, I learned of an old Italian saying: "If you love your children and want what's best for them, want them to be okay, see that their mom is okay."

And so, I started doing my part with more good-will and compassion. Which confused Janis at first. But little by little, we both started to change and open up. Though not romantically, we became closer and shared more, and one of those shared things was my poetry.

Janis worked in the publishing industry as a copywriter and editor, and she was good at it. But also, she was exceptional because of her creative intuition in editing and critiquing poetry. What a huge help and blessing she was, working in such harmony on three books of poetry, over the years.

One poem, a kind of bucolic everyday family-life poem, she said: "Gar, nice poem, all in all good, but there's a problem ... it makes you sound like such a nice regular guy. Let's be honest, you're not that nice a guy." Holy moly, there you go, priceless! So I changed the last of it, made it more honest.

Janis probably started her personal spiritual quest when she was a student at Columbia. Serious trauma in her family in Brooklyn stirred up, drove her to ask, as many of us have, "Why?" "Why and how can this be? And where is my place in all of it?"

The promise, so clean and clear, and almost within reach as youngsters, we find later fractured, bandaged, and suspect. Not at all resembling what held our undivided attention at an earlier time. Yet we can't give up on it, can we?

Over the years, Janis created a quiet, manageable life for herself in our original little Hoboken house. We shared some holiday dinners together. She was a thoughtful and interested hostess. Kept her Tea connection, meditation, and even Tai chi. And she was always full of smiles, ear to ear and eager, for visits from our Danny.

Janis, like so many of us, did her best. Her sudden, unexpected passing just came up and happened. How, why, don't ask me. But we were all with her at the last, sang a song, cried, and let her move on. Peace and a quiet harmony, her last gift to us.

I'll end with this from Janis: "When I was about to return home from Japan, Soen Roshi gave me a can of powdered tea and a tea whisk. He said, 'Make tea wherever you go.' This has been the spirit of my life ever since."

Thank you, dear Soshin-Janis.

I Have No Words

Under that hospital blanket, someone I know well, so well –
over forty years – now still.
Engulfed in solidarity, a richness, and a sadness,
not misery – more like amazement – its complexion.

Threading back through our journey, like whistle stops on a long
track.
Whistle stops within whistle stops, homes within towns of them.
Roses and arborvitae dot the yard, weeds and troublesome
plants here and there, even a small cedar, special and welcome,
seeded by the breeze.

Under a cream colored blanket, her recently combed hair, wisping out
at the edge.
I have no words, a brief chant – some music she enjoyed.
Engulfed we are, again.
A warmth, a completeness coming
arrives
and settles over us.

Dedication

Soen Nakagawa Roshi

Peggy Crawford and I jumped into the chilled waters of Beecher Lake every afternoon, that October. Our commitment was, we would take a swim every day, until the lake froze over, to show Soen Roshi how much, how badly we wanted him to come back and guide us, his sangha of Zen students here in the U.S.

A couple weeks later, we shimmied into the lake for the last time, through a thick layer of icy slush that would freeze solid that night. On the bank of the lake, watching us, a group of fellow Zennies, bundled up in winter coats, hats and scarfs.

That last dip was understandably short, but I remember looking up at our spectators, and cheerleaders, and saying to myself that they looked colder than we were.

Anyway, it didn't work, even through the slush, cold and our single-minded determination. Soen stayed secluded in Ryutaku-ji Monastery, Japan, and from his seclusion, those many miles away, he sent a powerful silent message, that some of us would carry with us even now, 48 years later: "Some guidance may come your way, but you are always and already home; yet you are the only ones to do the heavy lifting to get here."

Oh yeah, a real sweat. The whole world must be lifted and tilted over the edge, into THIS immutable moment.

*Wherever I go
is my home in eternity*
Soen Nakagawa Roshi

Acknowledgements

Can you believe this, a fourth book of Poems. As a trusted reader mentioned; "… and you are getting better."

Good to hear. It certainly is a labor from a special, lively, and gritty place, that I'm fond of visiting. (Or does it visit me?)

True, we work alone as artists, especially in the germination of it, but dearly count on, and depend on the good will, insight, and faith in us, of certain folks around us.

Let me once again express my deep gratitude to these friends, acquaintances, and family.

First, the late Janis Levine, whom this book is dedicated to. Her editing skills, insights, and conversations meant so much.

Then Justin Millan, his critiques of each and every poem made such an impact, just cut right through to the juice of it.

And the following readers for there observations and encouragement: Donna and Paul Marshall, Aurelia Navarro, Dale Erickson, Carolyn Pape, Eric Millan, Esther Aguilera, Xiaoqing Zhu, and my great friend for all these years, Peter Atkinson.

A special thanks to Kathryn Kimball, for suggesting "The Mole Penthouse," as the title, as well as her reading of the poems. Kathryn's gentle audacity and ability to see things afresh has been so valuable.

Huge appreciation goes, again, to my dearest sister, Gwendolyn Galsworth, for her consistent, enthusiastic support, hard work, and belief in the value of this poetry.

Then, of course Iwan Sujono, for his patience and skill in designing these books.

Lastly, with everlasting gratitude for Carol Millan, my wife, the bright intelligent yet soft light that shines on me, through all the ups and downs. With her, things get better, yet are complete and so worthwhile as they are.

Introduction

I'm not writing as many poems nowadays, and at times I wonder why? Maybe it's because there is less pain and struggle than there used to be. Or, maybe it's because pleasure and pain, struggle and harmony, are not so distant from one another anymore. Perhaps the Rockies and Grand Tetons are being smoothed out into the Catskills, as this flow of life passes over them.

Life's river, at times placid, mirror smooth, at times churning and full of the wild and the wilderness. Yet the source is always the same, a small spring bubbling up out of nowhere in particular, going nowhere in particular, complete in itself.

If I can, I want to find a way back to that source.

Remembering the words of Walt Whitman might help: "Lounge and the Muse will come." Or the words of a smart but more blunt character, my Pop: "So you're going on the bum again, are you?"

It's ironic isn't it, but also makes sense, if you want "art" to express itself, it needs room. Not unlike the squash and cucumber plants in our garden. Box'm in with too little space, too much purposeful activity, and the weeds and fencing chokes and stunts them.

Another way of seeing it ... being lost, searching for a way, even with some desperation, *creates*. Finding one's way to solid footing, a direction, getting secure, comfortable ... well, I don't know?

But I will say, my life in many ways has gotten better, much better. How? I simply find myself in the day I'm actually in more often. And that day is an okay day, a good day, a bright day even at 83 years.

The atmosphere of anticipated joy or trauma, expected acceptance or rejection, has thinned out, much of the time, to the point of transparency and invention.

An ancient Chinese Zennie said: "Imagination becomes experience."

My hope: As the poems of pain and loss found me, let the poems of "cease-fire" and harmony find me.

Table of Contents

ONE
A Childlike Repose

A Childlike Repose   2
Adobe   3
Back Around The Bend   4
Mid-March   5
After That   6
The Sapling   8
Mid-Day   10
Brings Me Back   11
Morning's Remnants   12
Never Them   13
DPs   14
Page Five   16
Chain-link   17
Nada   18
Cicadas   19
Shadows and Cardinals   20
The Thing About Crazy   21
The Weather   22
She Looks Up   23
The Bottom Shelves   24
The Doe   25
Again   26
Don't   27
Down Below   29
Institutionalized   30
Information Update   31
Late in the Day   32
Misplaced   33
In the Quiet   34
Why—Why Not?   35
Toby and the Ballet Slippers   36

TWO
All I Could Find

3:20 AM   40
A Steady Trickle   41
Offerings   42
Beat the Odds   43
Cowards and Heroes   44
Stand Still, Listen   45
Afternoon   46
December   47
Does One Wait?   48
Defies Belief   49
Is That The Secret   50
Nodding Off   52
The Mill   53
Last Night Gave Birth To Icicles Uncountable   55
Magic   56
In Passing   57
Nothing Itself   59
Looks That Way   60
After the Wine   62
One Heartbeat   63
Too Much   64
The Railing   65
One Day   66
The Folks   67
The Nudge   69
Just Enough   70
Yes/No   71
Why Ask?   72
All I Could Find   73

THREE
Iterations

Iterations   76
October   80
Paving Stones   81
The Familiar   82
Waiting   83
"The Sum of the Facts…"   84
Tunnel Vision   86
Notes and Coffee Stains   88
You Could Say That   89
One-Way Tickets   90
Take Your Time, But Hurry Up   92
Sidestepped   93
Aiming High   94
A Dwelling Place   95
The Edge   97
Dandelion Dreams   98
Small Talk   99
Just Right   100
Fred   101
A Touch of Defiance   104
Meandering   105
E.R.   107
Walking Past   108
Bulgaria   109
Trackless   110
Down At Debs   111
Yes My Dear   112
Carefully   114
Oh, the Humanity   115
Words   117
Worms   118
Seven Out of Ten   119

FOUR
Thank You Sir

Thank You Sir   122
Once Upon a Time   124
Afternoon to Evening   125
Confluence   126
Embers   127
Awakening   128
Closer to the Bone   129
Idyllic   130
Day After Day   131
Metronome   133
The Visitor   134
Not Allowed   135
Gripped in a Tight Fist   136
Pirouette   137
Tears and Drinks All Around   139
Just In Case   140
Yoshin's Forest   141
Unclaimed Baggage   142
Decks Awash   143
We'll Catch Them   144
Harvest Moon   146
Ground   147
Side By Side   148
Vespers   149
Wildflowers   150
That's Easy   151
Sisters   152
Fire Sale   153
Your Name? "…macht frei"   154
Revved   155

FIVE
The Mole Penthouse

An Easy Way Out   158
Boundaries   159
Making It Up   161
Mountain Bird   162
Morning Zen   163
Staying in the Game   164
Oil Found on the Moon   165
Unknowable   166
Think About It   167
Budapest   168
Chocolate Bar Love   169
Heartburned   170
Coho   171
Autumn Upon Them   174
And It Was True   175
Very Early   176
Black Robes   177
Runaway   178
Bittersweet   179
Love Prevailed   180
In Their Reflection   181
The Bluff   182
Your Face   183
A Garden   184
The Mole Penthouse, A Story   185

About Gary Galsworth   199

ONE

A Childlike Repose

A Childlike Repose

She looked quite beautiful in death.
Almost naked, peaceful, no pain, no torment.
In the time we were together, in that room
with drapes pulled closed around us,
she looked youthful, creamy smooth,
childlike in repose.

Decades earlier she'd looked like that,
almost naked, peaceful, complete,
after we made love.

I used to look for where things began,
and where they ended. Now I wonder
if there's a difference.

Adobe

A grasshopper clings to
the same wall I'm leaning on

absorbing the warmth
of a waning day

Back Around The Bend

Beyond the curve of the horizon
back around the bend
time stood still

On a busy highway
in the rush of traffic
racing my bike on the center line

Down a landing ship's ramp into a bottomless
blue-green sea
in an armored cocoon that went way under
before it very slowly floated up

The first time I ever asked you
out for coffee

In the delivery room
off to one side
very still

On a cushion in a dharma hall one night
when the detonation of links and senses
dissolved this world's connection

Awakened—to find myself
in the Alhambra
before it was a place or a name

And today
hearing you on the stairs
soft in your pale blue slippers

Mid-March

The evergreens were bent all to hell under this snowfall.
A sudden storm, thick, quiet, last night's dazzling.
I watched it floating through the streetlights,
went onto the porch, then down to the yard to feel it.

Snowflakes, plump and damp. For the minutes I stood among them,
their cold touch, a tease, a joy.
And then the added pleasure of moving back to shelter.
"Perfect, I should get my camera ... " which I didn't, but hung out
and watched the storm create a world with no sharp edges.

The next day, gardening in the snow drifts, walking around the
property, saving my bent, almost breaking evergreens,
knocking off the heavy snow with a broom.
Looks like they are ok, almost, most of them. We'll see.
Only two broken branches so far.

And that should be it for this winter.
But as my neighbor says, "You never know anymore."
I'll bet his great grandfather said the same thing mid-March,
last century.

After That

Completely dependent but ignorant of our predicament;
isn't that a form of freedom?
We begin to sort it out, and little by little,
dependency diminishes.
On the surface at least.
Our cells still need water, salt, an assortment of things.
On the surface, the sensory realm, we get some flex.
In the arc of it, we wean ourselves off this wall-to-wall
neediness, and achieve some wiggle room.
Autonomy on the level of mass transit, lunch,
perhaps some kisses, better schools for the kids.

Dependency sprouting independence, our appetite grows,
and we're starting to start accumulating.
Hardware, software, loungewear, work wear—commitments,
loyalties, longings, a lover's underwear.
Flypaper-mind grows up.
Soon we need to put a roof over it, a garage, fences,
destinations …
And so, independence loaded—clinging, have-to-have's,
got-to-be's, hugs, perpetual hard-ons, and the attendant financing.
Paralyzed in worry—smothered in gummy ambition.

Dependency on the rise, but mental. Where to find mental?
Go ahead, look.
Have a good look.

Though unseen, the arc of all this is inexorable, way ahead of us,
and carries innate solutions.
As the zenith is crested and we move on, we find we can't manage
this web of connections, and still carry our own golf clubs.
Simplification must follow, through swollen ankles, bone spurs,
and gaps in our synapses.

On this end—this other end of the rainbow, dependent again.
But we are less and less aware of our predicament,
and isn't that a form of freedom?

The Sapling

My father planted a small sapling when he started building
the new house for his new family.
I'm sure he felt good about marking that.
He worked hard painting houses, and the pay was poor.
Being able to build your own place on your own property was
no little thing, for him, for his wife,
and their numerous children.

Not long ago I was taken there for the first time.
The house is a small brick ranch, one floor and a garage.
In the front yard is the sapling, now an elegant tree, very tall.
A beautiful tree.
One of those tall slender oaks that grow in Georgia.
In the sun and the breeze, it celebrates.
It celebrates everything; after all it's summer.

The house is still in place, needing some TLC.
My father's descendants, squatting there, don't seem moved to
give it much.
Available cheap shelter for busy lives.
Lives where the months are generally a day too long
and a dollar short.
It's a different time, a different world.
One with less gardening and maintenance, and more backlit
screens and big plans.
Big plans based on over-stimulated imaginations and
too much sugar.
Backlit screens, of all sizes, sucking the juice out of the room.
Well, no one is complaining but me, and the roof is still good.

Back home now, it's October, cool, and grey.
There's a stiff breeze, and you can hear it making a different sound in the oaks than in the maples.
I know this same breeze passed across the shingles of my father's sturdy house, and through that tall tree in Georgia.
Celebrating still, perhaps just life itself.
Mine, my father's—scattered lives, yet connected, continuous, regardless of the content, or how one measures it.

Mid-Day

Koi flash across our little pond
sunlight dressing and undressing them.
Leaves and shadows drift past.

A fish breaks the surface gulping bubbles.

I'm on the patio, blending into a chair,
and a book.
Carol is in the house doing chores in her pajamas:

This day's ticket to freedom.

Brings Me Back

Sounds of water trickling
under ice and snow
and the humidity deep inside
a hooded parka
bring me back
to lying on summer's grass
looking at night skies
waiting for the streak and fall
of a star

Morning's Remnants

dew drops

on bamboo

Never Them

I used to cast my net to catch
all the butterflies

Later
one or two would do

Now I wait on
our appointment

Even if it's never them
or never you

DPs

In Georgia, walking a sandy old logging road.
Woods on either side, hardwoods, pines, puddles from yesterdays heavy rain.
The woods get dense up ahead, and fill in to the edge of the road.

Into my more or less empty head comes fantasy images and foggy associations from the war. World War Two, Germany,
Eastern Europe.
Sandy wooded roads leading to big personal problems.

Our teacher, in fourth grade, called us to attention: *"Children please. Sit down for some news."*
Our school, and our class were going to be getting DPs.
Children from Europe who would find new homes here.
A ship of DPs had arrived and our town was getting some.

DPs was the name for Displaced Persons, our teacher explained.
The terrible war in Europe had left many people, families and children, with no homes and no schools, and a lot of struggles to just get by.
We were trying, she said, here in the USA, to help out and offer them a better future.

The DPs were quiet children, well groomed, and worked hard in school, on their grades and projects.
They were kids, so after the first days of us gawking, (coached by our teachers to behave normally and treat them the same), and them wide-eyed, we all started blending together, just about.
They remained a little different. Not enough to be excluded from anything, but they were neater and more attentive, and not smooth.
We American kids, though different nationalities; mainly Italian, Polish, Jewish, Black, and poor White, there was a smoothness in our features

Like an American layer of soft flesh (Not fat, kids weren't
fat back then).
The DPs didn't have that.
Their features and demeanors were delineated, taut.
You could see their origins.
You could see hints of history and personal experience we had
no inkling of, could not have dreamed of on our worst nights.

Arny Rosenthal from Latvia. Tiia Aavkauk from Estonia.
No one we knew had names like that.
We saw their little countries on our map in school.
Tiia, slim, pale, ice blue eyes, her pretty, unusual face had a
trace of Asian in it.
She made friends easily, and her mother was always at the
edge of the playground to meet her after school.
In those days, a quaint thing to do. We all just scattered,
on bikes, or walking, to go home on our own.

Tiia, slim, pale, ice blue eyes, she was the first unusual beauty
that I needed to make a part of my life. A ten-year old life.

It played out, especially any successes, only in my head.
In spite of a true-believers earnestness, my efforts were limited
by not even knowing where to begin.

One is tempted to peer into the future, her future, now long past.
Track it.
Then I see her mother at the playground's edge,
school just letting out, waiting.

Page Five

On page five of the book I'm reading
there is a stain along the bottom edge.
Mayonnaise from a little piece of egg salad that slid off
my cracker.

In the future, some reader reading this book,
will get to the bottom of page five, and notice that old stain.

Our reader of the future might have a thought along the lines of:
What is that?
Who made it?
When?
He will probably never guess it was me;
two days before another birthday, up late reading,
and eating celebratory crackers and egg salad.

Probably not.

Chain-link

It hasn't been a great year for poems. They turn up now and then,
like a rabbit in the grass out back. I can't explain it.
Perhaps because, aside from this damned head cold,
things have been okay.
No broken hearts, no fingers crushed in doors slammed by others.
My bones and cartilages are even pleased, since I stopped
working like Sisyphus, whether I needed to or not.

Even got a nice girl. Really. We have interesting conversations,
two and three days in a row, over meals or a walk,
without crisis or the miseries.
When we kiss, she makes a little sound that can only mean
it's part of her dream-come-true too.
Sometimes I kiss her in front of people, lightly and affectionately
of course, it's public, and I'm old.
But folks get a kick out of it, young women sigh,
friends hide a smile.

Not long ago, last year it was, I sold my brownstone.
If I had waited till this week, I'd have made a bundle more.
But, would I have gotten to that long meditation retreat last fall?
The one where I resolved to let the fencing fall away,
or drop dead trying.
The fencing did fall away—but resurrected.
And I didn't drop dead, or if I did, it went undetected.

More porous boundaries, chain-link to split rail, will do for now.
And a poem or two moved into the space occupied by that
antique brownstone.
I'd rather not give them back for a better deal.

Nada

Look at me, sturdy as they come.
Not stronger than my fears though,
which have no bones, no pulse,
no nada.

Just a child's story, told on the porch
after sunset.
Kinda fun, kinda scary,
nothing much driven by
nothing at all.

Cicadas

Cicadas and
there's a quarter moon

Shadows and Cardinals

Branches cast shadows
and the current plays them

A distant birdsong takes
me to a cardinal I cannot see

And stream sounds murmur the edge
off a too strong cup of coffee

The Thing About Crazy

The thing about crazy people is they think it's true.
They think what they see and hear so clearly, and understand
with such conviction, is true.
For us outside that truth, we see with our hearts and our
knotted guts, that it ain't going to work.
And it ain't going to be fun, but be pain and struggle.
A struggle with a heavy hand, the blunt heavy hand of our world,
which asks so much of us,
maybe too much.

The thing about crazy people is we want to love them, help them,
fix them.
And they want our love, our possibility of safety, refuge,
but at times they are so nuts, where does one begin?
At times it's just convincing the cops they don't need their hands
on their guns.
*Believe me sir, please, she's harmless, just swearing and yelling;
she's scared out of her wits.*

A real sweat.

How many heads can one juggle?
Not anymore than we have to.

The Weather

It's snowing tonight.
Maybe the same over there, where they keep him.
The old man.
He's out of it, he don't know from much anymore
—a vegetable, asleep most of the time.

Tomorrow Gaitan will visit. He'll wear a nametag, his name
printed large.
When he's at the bedside he'll cradle the old man's head,
whose mouth will hang open a bit, as they do.
As his head is lifted, he'll open his eyes and see "Gaitan"
on his son's nametag.

And he'll light up, as the connection, the sparks, and pathways
flag each other, spin around for a moment or two,
and finally embrace a nameless contentment.

The snow will probably continue all morning.

She Looks Up

If your mom loves you
(goes without saying most times)
it's also good if she's short.
You look down at her she looks up at you.
Makes you feel like a big man. *A mensch.*
I'm a smallish guy but never felt
that way.
Big ideas, big mouth, big convictions.
Big mistakes now and then.

With the right mom, it's never your fault.
A mensch.

The Bottom Shelves

I don't want to be like this, in the clutter, and the sticky heat.
Not again.
The shelves in the front room are crammed with books.
Old magazines are collecting dust.
And what's with this keeping of books upon books, already read,
or never will be?
Like someone on high is keeping track, nodding approval.

You're stuck aren't you, collecting dust and dead cells?
And you can't turn your skin back in, even though it's on loan.
There is a desire for the tidy, and low humidity, and sincere
welcomes that do not turn into moldy stories looking for a
fresh pair of ears.

Anonymity is big-hearted—*time is not.*
We had some good days awash in it.
Sunny, babies on the beach smiling, sand clinging to every fold.
Why are they smiling, and they are, even at me.
Contentment in different shades and colors, awash in it.

That was before I got so fussy.

The Doe

A doe wandered onto our gravel road

Paused looked around then took another cautious step

Dignified elegant and perfectly ignorant

Again

Shadows reach out nab my hair
cut my throat
A fixed grin beams at the rubber knives
of childhood

Why this struggle
Let withered leaves fall away
Why this call to answer the door

Don't

Don't get caught
daydreaming,
taking a nap—
or looking into the other room halfway through
the evening meal, like that's where you'd rather be.

And don't get caught having an expectation,
God forbid,
that you really expect to happen.
"Please Mr. Man, can you somehow make sure?"

Don't get caught planning to—
run away,
plead innocent,
trying to get more wiggle room.
And don't wiggle!
If I can't, you can't!

Don't get caught enthusiastically
looking for love,
or expressing it,
in hopes of rescue.
"Watch your valuables; another bunch of immigrants,
just got off the boat, starry-eyed, and nervous."

Don't get caught thinking
with your face,
averting your gaze,
not waiting your turn.
And don't get caught trying to understand; ponder
forbidden questions—you know better.
You better.
Wondering why it's all so sticky?

Don't … turning your back,
switching off the light,
making believe
no one is home
but you.

Down Below

Down below worms are busy
Not those kind of worms
I mean regular—you know earth worms
they eat dirt munch munch

While up here rock bands go ape-shit and SUVs
tool around like
they own the place

Munch—a large rat I've seen bigger but not much—
makes a break for it
Just before skipping into the bushes he checks for predators
and edibles

Under constellations of recessed lighting
scorning the possibility of worms and other dirt eaters
I make myself comfortable in the airport terminal
A youngster about 9 years old shares a row of seats with me
He seems compelled to rock back and forth—back and forth—and
snap a plastic coffee lid
Snap SNAP
His mom is not unsettled

How does one respond
Is one to make an issue of—snap Snap rock rocking munch
munch Munch?

Institutionalized

They don't care here. No one is listening, no one is looking.
It's okay.
In peripheral vision I see him, but his attention is elsewhere.
Listen to the sound.
The sound of rain running down the gutter-spout.
Stand still under the eaves. Cozy, calm.
Take your time finishing your coffee.
It's okay.
There's a man at the end of the driveway, but he's walking away, toward the road.
Probably going to the mailbox.
I'm thousands of miles from home. Won't be any mail for or about me.
It's okay.
But I don't know, not so sure about this.

Information Update

You may be wondering why we haven't started again.
Found a place, some place, almost any place, to gather and abide
in silence, share the peace, the completeness in non-creation.
Or just ruminate as one shifting collection of grey matter.

It's because I've been attending to life's other business.
Sitting in hospital cafeterias while upstairs a loved one
struggles and trusts.

Also been hauling boxes of clothes, dishes, and stuff from one
place to another.
Again?
So soon?
Fine.
Next?
Fixing a broken down handtruck that hardly seemed worth it,
'till my back gave me updated information.

We'll find a way to be in the same room again, quietly;
right now the noise of life calls.
I could run away into silence or into more comforting murmurs,
but that would happen only if I expected better answers there.
Plus, I'm in it for her weak smile, as she feels a little better,
and a plate of spaghetti in the hospital cafeteria.

Late in the Day

A breeze passes leaves descend
like flights of sparrows come to feed
and scatter
Sunlight bending over them

Misplaced

Lost by others
found by others
I went along for the ride

For Carol

In the Quiet

This place could be a bungalow, or a trailer,
in the hills somewhere.
Let's say southeast Kentucky or the Catskills of New York.
This morning I heard rain coming off the roof.
Got up, pee'd, ate a couple crackers.
Sounds from a distant neighbor filtered in, and the birds.

The highs and lows of the day, similar to the peaks and valleys
that surround me, becoming more alike with time,
not changing much.
Plenty to do, the days are too short, but urgency is rare.
A natural movement, tai chi-like, stepping across the hours.

The grass is getting high. Soon it'll be a bear to cut.
Note that, but don't make trouble out of nothing.
There is plenty to do in nothing, as it is.

Why—Why Not?

Sometimes on my own I don't
eat
Sometimes on my own I don't
sleep
Sometimes on my own I run
and run—delighting in it
And sometimes I ask: why look
farther than this

Toby and the Ballet Slippers

Younger I had more time.
Time for elaborate plans, most of which went nowhere.
That in itself probably saved my life more than once.
And time for the unexpected. Which took up a lot, an era or two.
And went where?
I mean, appointments were made and kept. Business partners, acquaintances, lovers, giving way to births, assistantships, museums, the night shift, knees to the groin, busted faces, busted credit, monumental traffic jams, life in a gridlock of its own.

Though not without its moments: high fives, as we beamed, clapped, and sighed with happiness.
Also streams of hospital visits, state and private, lithium at 3 pm on the third floor, birthday parties with no guests, and birthday guests waiting, wondering.
No problems that couldn't be raged at, or swamped with indefatigable longing.

Yes, plenty of time for all that.

When the kid was four, I walked around the block, Jackson Heights, and Pied Piper'd neighborhood kids back to the house.
"Hey, you want to come to a birthday party?
Go ask your Mom if it's okay?"
A big success.
Ours, the birthday girl, dancing in her new ballet slippers.
Plenty of time, much more than now, to spend like a lottery winner.
Because I was, you know, *A Life*.

Now it's wall-to-wall errands and this week I have to clean the house, or she might not show up.
Spied dust bunnies under the dresser and under the bed.
Dust, sweep, mop, and for god-sakes—vacuum: who has time for that? I already have a job, and am getting better at it. It's not to let my extremism, the need to make every move count, and then hold others accountable for the gaps; not to let that take over the management.
My real job: to not create that familiar space, gridlock followed by a nosedive.

My good friend Peter trains dogs. Big ones. He's strict, but in his way, a loving taskmaster.
For us, well there was Toby, our Labrador; we would drive her to the park for a run. One of our joys. A great dog.
Funny, so many great dogs.
People say, "a great dog." And it's always true.
Arriving home we discovered Toby was not in the back of the truck. We'd left her in the park.
How?
My God, how does one do that? Three wacky miles, driven in fear and remorse, to find her sitting at the curb of a big Chicago intersection, waiting.
Happy, calm, timeless.
And it all came to nothing, just as it's supposed to—I guess.

See, part of me is still suspicious, still ambitious, still bent on creating something special.

Today I've got to water the annuals hanging on the porch.
And the ferns.
It's been a good early fall for the ferns, green and abundant.
The annuals are starting to get that worn look, but from my seat I see yellow flowers. And across the lawn deep red ones.
All thirsty.

One wins the Life Lottery, and no matter what it comes to, probably nothing much, we get to hear an occasional breeze sweep the trees, and recall Toby waiting at the curb.

TWO

All I Could Find

3:20 AM

*clap clap
ching!*

Pale teacup icy cold
draws the heat from
my fingers

Shoji bows

Returns it
amber
and steaming

*clap clap
ching!*

A Steady Trickle

Shouldn't I be somewhere else
doing more than sharing
this peace and quiet

Working hard
on things that need to be done

Looking at the streambed a steady trickle
passing through the sand and pebbles
I see everything that needs doing is being done

Offerings

I know a fellow who writes, calls himself a poet.
He owns a small greengrocery: fresh fruits,
vegetables, homemade pies.

I know him well, and the real poems, the ones with heart,
are in the way he handles his apricots, his strawberries, and
tomatoes.
The way he offers them to you.

How he looks at his amber and resilient wife as she passes,
stocking shelves, arranging flowers for display.
He looks at her all businesslike and serious,
but his eyes can't hide the poetry of his affection.

Beat the Odds

Crush your clock.
Okay, don't. If it were only that easy.
Face it to the wall; you'll enjoy some brief relief
before your stomach knots up.

Might get a kick out of that experience,
hearing the tick tock tick tock
of a clock without hands

The clickety clack, the whoosh, the gurgle,
the seamless unbroken parade.
What float will you ride on, what marching band,
or band of pipers will you step in with?

Carried across the arc of this day,
like it was another day whose content
made a difference.
Its contents, me, stretching between
events that are none other than myself.
Sunup, pillows, and blankets, and fighting off the need
to get up and pee.
Morning, a phone call and a bagel; soggy but all I got.
Noon and afternoon, jeans over pj's to move the car and come
back in to type some things of historical impotence.

Still resonating a special sensibility that, recreating
experience, and penetrating the webs of time,
ruminates endlessly about—itself.
At the end of this day's arc, sore from sitting too long,
my day has barely started. Contents generating contents.
Crank up Ray Charles and see if I can beat the odds.

Cowards and Heroes

Four of us enjoying the beach, swimming in the Gulf,
on spring break.
Toby, her boyfriend John, Fred Henson (we always called him
Fred Henson, like it was one word: Fredhenson), and myself.
Then—the sharks swam up.

Amid the frenzy of splashing to escape, cowards and heroes
were revealed.
We raced off, frantic to get away.
John and Toby towards the beach, Fred and I towards the
big grey rocks of a jetty.
John made sure he stayed between the sharks and Toby.
Shielding her, you could see, till they struggled onto the beach,
his arm around her waist.

Fredhenson and I swam like madmen alongside each other.
He was between me and the sharks.
I prayed they would hit him first. Then maybe I'd have a chance.
Maybe I could make it!
We reached the jetty, scrambled up the slick rocks, bruising
and scratching ourselves on barnacles, but we didn't care.

Later, all huddled on our blanket, sipping beer, reliving it.
A guy came along walking his golden retriever.
We started sharing our tale.
He interrupted. "No sharks; dolphins. No sharks here; dolphins."
and walked on.

Stand Still, Listen

A car passing, muted.
A truck passing, coarse, wearing in its determination, softening in the distance.
A Harley bangs by, boisterous, busting through the quiet so we'd all be the first to know.
A brook, its sounds of passage soothing, healing.

Stand still, listen.

My passing, footfalls soft on moss.
A bird hears, chirps the news.
The breeze, stirring the hair on my neck.

Tonight, looking at the moon, the sound of breathing, barely audible.
Was it the moon, or that solitary firefly weaving through the grass nearby?

Afternoon

A whole afternoon moves through these fingertips
stroking your hair
soothing your temples
hardly stirring

The city
all its stress and animation falls quiet
as your head
rests on my chest

December

Raining, though looking into the grey sky I don't see it.
All just flat and chilly.
Shifting my gaze to the big cedar in our yard,
and there's the rain.
Silver streaks, flashing past dense green branches.
December rain, stepping outside,
I welcome its sting.

Does One Wait?

At some stage names began to form, forms and
shapes began to introduce themselves.
Which led me to believe I could tell what I was looking for.
Hope in different colors, palpable expectations.
Though it rubbed ragged and wore thin, I never tired of the quest.

Coming through the high weeds, past the tangles,
pressing back the reeds that open to a pond. Very still, warm,
a green film covering its surface.
Teeming with birds and insects, sun glistening off their quick
movements.
All here, of a piece, and still secret.
Surprised; I had come to expect inevitable change,
and its aftertaste.

Now, sitting on the porch, feeling the flow of seasons,
I'm less inclined to wait on the wheel's turning, and less
inclined to put my shoulder in to it.

Defies Belief

Stuck in that place where you believe in love
as an approved narcotic.
In whose embrace, in the glow of which,
salvation and meaningful answers lie.
I keep returning to the same back room
of the same secondhand bookstore,
looking for treasure.
That priceless first edition.

See that smiling little girl, with a down-at-the-heels mom.
She doesn't have a clue but knows where she wants to be,
and that all is well.
Someday she'll grow up, maybe put two and two together.
Can't say I ever have.

Think about the travails of other treasure hunters.
Their problems come after a find.
Going through all that work, the privations, frustrations,
dry holes; to finally score, ring the brass bell.
It gets them wrecked, or killed, guard down—in wonderment.

Is That The Secret

I've come to believe a little
in innocence
But how could you
All of them?
Erased
They were only—participating
in—the unquantifiable
A birdman's shuffle
You quantified them qualified and
disqualified them
Nonsense silly dreadful
I find it impossible to accept
Unacceptable
You'll have to anyway
or you won't get far before you're parched
and shriveled
Hey—don't you also find that impossible to accept
Don't then—squirm and stew in it
or is it painless dumbed down
anesthetized in clouds of conviction
But how—was no one home
Is that the secret—vacate the premises
Well perhaps
Absolution in amnesia absentia
or a simple change of focus
Street people know something about ducking
and weaving
about managing a day unplugged
Ask them how it's done

How mashed potatoes at Boston Market offered
more solace and redemption for Mimi than worlds of
treatment and therapy
She was innocent
Almost completely—no one cares anymore
Except I do—still do
Who to share that with
Is anybody out there?
Anyone not armed to the teeth
Feeling the thump thump the pulse
in our own fingertips makes us seem less perishable
We lost the house—I couldn't save it
Our child seems at loose ends wandering
Stepping stones turn cul-de-sacs
We never lost each other

Nodding Off

After nodding off I raised my head to see a jumble of
people nearby.
Aware, but I was still in that space before time and place
come back together.

As my waking self re-constitutes a life, I realize those
people are a group of dolls from someone else's childhood,
propped up in the corner.
Behind them, outside our big window, a tumble of leaves,
casting a dance of shadows.

When I open my eyes again, it's quiet.
A doll baby is sitting upright with raised arms, and raised hands,
in 70 years of stillness.
And I can hear the river, spilling over the falls.

The Mill

I'm looking out at the woods
at an old factory visible through the trees
A clock tower
Sprays of green
Sprays of countless buds on countless branches
change in the endless wheel of seasons

that ceaseless play

What shall we do in it
Let's sit on the couch and decide—about today
You start

As we're finally getting the hang of things
we come to understand
this does not go on and on
changes have an end—will finish
all of it
for us as we are

There is a sadness in that a flattening effect
A wall prickly with apprehension and inequity
can start to build
one miserable brick at a time

Hearing the shower running
bathing one's love in all her trust
and vulnerability
one sees we must find a place outside of
what starts and what finishes
Tuck ourselves into it
Do we have another choice—it's the only choice I see

Looking at the clock tower—old and hard in granite's
mute conviction
rising above sprays of pale green—fresh fragile
stirring in the sunlight
But all sewn with the same needle the same thread
That ceaseless play

And what shall we do in it
Come let's sit on this bench and decide about today
You start

Last Night Gave Birth To Icicles Uncountable

Luminous against the endless evergreens,
bough upon bough, branch beyond branch, snowy curtains
and chorus lines of them.

The wind sings, cedars bend, brittle cascades rain to ground,
scattering in crystal splashes.

Sunlight; droplets blue and pure,
trickle down fingers of ice and stillness.

For Sis (Gwen)

Magic

Stirring my tea
sets this forest spinning
and all its leaves are peppermint

In Passing

In the corridor, coming off the escalator, she walked past.
I'd say mid to late thirties, maybe forty. I'm bad at that,
but she smiled in passing, and her presence drew me in.

She was not tall and not slim, but looked perfect in her way,
with her hair pulled back in a ponytail, plain, light brown.

Not slim does not mean overweight, as in, "Oh, he likes heavy
girls." I'd have to say I like them all, if they have a certain look.
Lord knows the origins of that—chemistry, DNA; and let's not go
into details, it just warps the conversation.

What's important is the "drawing in," and the fact that I nearly
turned around to catch up, ask her for a moment, a chat.
Can I make your acquaintance?
Do something other than let her pass to the past.

Maybe it would have taken off, taken flight,
become a treasure hunt.
If you could see me you'd see how odd all that would be.
But you can't and that's not a bad thing.

See, I can't just give up.
At least not in the inner recesses of my head. Way in back.
Even though a familiar look says almost nothing of the content.
And in my life, the content can be a tar baby; often is.
And that's got to be okay too, how do you give back a *tar baby?*

I know a mom, with two grown sons. One took such careful tough
love, such vigilant nurturing to get grown, through school, and
into a respectable job. It was touch and go, but they, as a family,
though mainly the mom, did it. Hurray, and thank you Lord!
"We got him launched."

Recently he met a neurotic, self-absorbed, hillbilly beauty down
south, his first real girlfriend. They're engaged now.
The mom is worried that all her projections and grooming are
going to go to shit.
I told her not to bother worrying, that's what's gonna happen,
for sure.
See, the kid is stunned by his luck, gaga, pussy whipped,
and happier than he's ever been.
Yes, there is often a price to pay, and he'll pay it, gladly.
Call me warped, a little twisted, but I'm happy for him.

Inside my chest there's a small hope brewing:
maybe I'll see her again,
and this time....

Nothing Itself

You want to know.
We all do.

How badly—badly enough to get a one-way ticket
and—get aboard?
Badly enough to bet all your chips, every last one?

Go ahead, make that move.

Oblivion holds no issues, no misery.
The prospect holds them all.

Takes ambition. The hungries,
mindless determination.
Risking everything, even your life?

—*If I have to*—
You will.

You still want to know?

Take that path through the pines,
there's a meadow, brambles,
and honeysuckle.

A butterfly can only tell the truth.

Looks That Way

Are you going to stay out there
forever
Looks that way
I wanted to share these moments
Too bad
I can still taste it you know
There's a hint of salt
Still hear it
High-pitched
but pleasant soothing
And the feeling—smooth
firm very soft
How come I got confused
My body knew
clear
simple
anonymous
Your world couldn't see that
offer any support even a little
Well maybe it did
Confusion is not defeat
rejection is not indifference
You had more important things to do
Safer
He said—I lost my voice
Not defeat but a hard row
and you can't rush it
Forever
sure looks that way

Sometimes I wonder
only for a minute anymore
what got missed neglected—overwhelmed
under stroked
Affection's tenacity
The affliction of mothers and other supplicants
Now then
out of my work boots into these ratty slippers
Always a perfect fit

After the Wine

We had a comfortable meal in a small restaurant.
She had a glass of red wine, drank about half.
Later in our hotel room she lay on the bed
and the tears started.
Before long, a deluge.
Distressing, painful.
Poor thing, she'd been keeping it inside, unheard, in check
for so long.
Eternities.
Feeling safe, the logjam broke and relief began to flow.
She cried and cried, and then she fell asleep.
It threw me off, but it seemed not a bad thing.
A gift of sorts, trusting me enough, to let me hear her cry
from her soul.

One Heartbeat

One heartbeat is
all we get
Soaked in life
missing nothing

Too Much

I loved you too much
How can I live and you not
The hunger of loss fills me
enough to attack your death
and snatch you back

But then we'd have to do this all again

Let me just sit here eyes closed
See the two of us

Before we started the house you made this bench
faced it toward that mountain we called our own
Working hard we'd rest on it
my leg touching yours

That leisurely persistent way of ours
now clotted in time

Perhaps it is myself I love too much
else I'd make the leap
a leopard's leap
and snatch you back

The Railing

Through the spindles of the porch railing
I see the driveway,
rain splashing on puddles.

Beyond those slender posts,
lined up in lean precision,
an unruly afternoon.

One Day

One day they'll come for him and haul what's left away.
Then someone else will come and nose through stuff.
Read a page, take in a letter, remark on a picture, a lamp,
or, "This guy sure had a lot to say. An opinion on everything."
Hey, is this an antique?
And that old shopping bag of drawings… cans of loose change…
And who'd have guessed he had so many pairs of shoes.

Then there's the rest—
Him sitting quietly in the front room, drinking bergamot tea out of a glass jar.
One of a set of mason jars his son sent, after he explained, complained, how that morning his jar had cracked.
Sitting, sipping, listening to the sounds outside.
Birds, the wind, morning people closing doors, driving off.

Listening to small sounds inside, house sounds as it heats and cools, lifts and settles.
Sitting quietly, listening to the sounds of his own inner works.
Webs of thought, colorful meanderings, passing breath,
and those many processes within, as they—expand and contract.

Listening to, sensing, the flowing clouds of matter that life had clothed him in.

The Folks

Look, they gave us a home to come home to, and most of the time
our own rooms.
And they owned the house we called our house.
We couldn't know the importance of that at the time;
one of those building blocks, of which we got many, even if the
packaging was often rough and blunt.
Later on, we'd have to do the building up, the heavy lifting,
the tearing apart, the walking (or running) away.
And—the coming back.

What else? Well, we got a Christmas tree, religiously a day or two
before, when they were cheaper, selling off the leftovers.
We put the skimpy side towards the wall.
And the tree was always laden with decorations, assorted bulbs,
some treasured till they fell and broke. The best and oldest bulbs
seemed unfairly to be most fragile.
A special ornament for the top, angel's hair and masses of tinsel;
a master's touch, Mom's, in a Brooklyn matzo ball sort of way.
Under the tree, plenty. Mom and even Sis and I, at some point,
belonged to the Christmas Club at the savings bank.
But Mom, a true believer, was at the teller's window with her
first small deposit, getting ready for next year (and not alone)
a week after the holiday.

Sometimes what you wished for really happened.
That was awesome.
Yes! I got the bow and arrow—with perfect target arrows!
Dreams come true!
A pattern one tries to replicate later.
And that can get pretty twisted.

After growing up, moving away, and creating, with time,
good health and perseverance, an unimaginable mess of it,
they welcomed me back, gave me time and a place to get on
my feet again, even with the setbacks, and later trusted me
with everything.
Helped lay a path for the possibility of a viable future, a refuge;
while across the moat, a wilderness of discord and ignorance
ebbed and flowed.
A waste, of toxic treasures carefully masked but lethal,
noxious junk, unconditional conviction; you name it.

Their goodwill never ended, although Pop, rolling his own smokes
that wouldn't stay lit, got struggly as he got ancient, more so than
he usually was.
Mom never shut us out, even as her body shut her down.
In her heart did she even notice how hard the journey?
Bodies bend, do hearts or souls bend, if they are not bent already?

In the last of it, seemingly unconscious, she waited till we all
arrived and could complete this family thing.
Waited till we were all accounted for.
She could feel the added warmth of our souls as we entered
her room; and then she left.

The Nudge

On the path, a silver beetle.
I bent down to move him so he wouldn't get stepped on.
After a nudge—*too late.*
Too late for him, I said.

Too late for what?

Too late for whom?

Just Enough

Two women in light summer dresses.
They changed the mood, the complexion of things,
just enough to create a handful of lively carnal mysteries.
The shape of their shoulders and backs through the fabric.
The way the material, pleated here and there,
flowed over their hips.
Bouquets enlivened with my own fancies, to pick and choose.

Should we meet, have a seat, a chat, I'd likely find slim pickings.
Bouquets seeded with wildflowers, roses not shorn of thorns.
Life's wear and tear.
Just enough myopia to turn expected romance into unexpected,
but inevitable misery.

An old man's carnal dreams, much like a young man's carnal dreams.

Yes/No

Yes
I'll get going, lots to do.

No
I'll sit here, very quiet, not moving.

A difference?

Why Ask?

It was today, in the dentist chair, looking at my friend the
dentist, her body turned away from me,
that I realized my body needs other bodies.
Near.
Somewhere near.

I am not sure how much I need this body, with its crampy legs,
and arthritic knees, but why ask?
Our bluff gets called soon enough on that.
But your body and mine, now there's a dance with some
good news in it.

All I Could Find

Hurting

I went looking for signs of death

for a dead girl

All I could find were signs of life

THREE

Iterations

Iterations

The last time I saw you your eyes were deep green,
perhaps from excitement.
And your jeans were…
—It comes to me that that morning was in fact a picture of the
memory of that morning from the last time I had thought about it.
I think of you every day, and it's been years.
Each picture another layer, and each layer changed a little.
A hair's breadth.
From then till now El Niño and our own restless minds have
circled the globe over and over, ever changing.
So many evenings, perfect ones as well, cicadas, a setting sun
catching the cedars, tea on the porch, a breeze—
Why, I remember an especially moving—but then—memories of
memories, each overlapping the last.
An original under the layers somewhere?
Perhaps.
Perhaps a green tint still highlights your eyes as you pass
into view.
Found where?

I decided to go back, through the layers. Better said, a decision
was made, something clicked and the exploration began.
Spelunking in that vast underworld array.
Cherished experiences slumbering in submerged subcutaneous
rooms.
Lodged somewhere in a vast yet commonplace geology.
We expect to rediscover them fleshed out, light- or dark-eyed,
interested and awaiting our arrival.
God forbid our torch illuminates an assortment of bones and
tendons, scraps of funk and hair.
The charnel house grin of someone who could wait no longer.

Finding we are all alone in a place that neither remembers
nor forgets.

Should have brought an extra sweater, a scented handkerchief.
You pick it up, but do you really want to re-read that letter?
That old letter, a redundancy of impassioned words,
uniquely directed at only you.
Dry, bittersweet recollections, more alike than different from
ones found scattered on ledges, in crannies elsewhere.
Catacombs, each niche holding its special secret, and its
selection of ordinary tibias.

I went down five hundred layers to find you, your brown hair
still highlighted here and there. And your smile recognizable.
Then, one thousand thin layers, and you spoke to me.
How nice to hear your voice, even though I was rattled by it.
Compelled, I leafed through more, eons of geology,
and came upon us climbing a hill through a meadow.
Clarity, center frame, fading and flawed around the edges.
You are walking up ahead, your jeans snug and denim blue
against your hips

You are turning and speaking as we walk, your skin pale
against a halo of years.
We're heading up the ridge and across a couple of hills to a
little valley where moonshiners, when you were a child,
had a still.
Reaching the old hilltop in love's playful time.
That time before the business of love sets in,
with its business ups and downs.

After walking the path awhile, I said, "What happens if I
collapse up here? Have a heart attack or something.
You can't carry me back, even for a farm girl."

And I sprawled on the path on my back, arms thrown out,
grass and weeds tickling my neck.
Funny guy.
I knew she'd come up with something. Knew she'd save me.
"Well," she said, "I'll just have to grab you by the ankles and
spin you around and drag you along, like one of those Indian
pole sleds."

Smiling, she did that. Stooped down, put one leg on either side
of her hips and started dragging me along.
I pretended to be unconscious, with some comments.
She played Indian girl, rescuing her warrior.
Sounds meaty and verdant, but it's just a barely lucid hint here
and there, distinct fragments amid the blur and slag.
My pockets, upended, started emptying.
Loose change, dimes and quarters tinkling onto the trail.
Can't you just hear them? Keys, my glasses.
And I flashed on how incongruous loose change and keys were,
spilling onto a trail where two lovers looking for an old still
had morphed into a faithful squaw saving her fallen warrior.
I guess we both saw it because she turned and started laughing.
Her laugh was a young girl's laugh, pure and high-pitched.
When I heard it, it hurt.
Pain managed to find a way through the loam.
Then I let the layers slip; slip away, till we got back to an aged
daguerreotype, spotted, blurred and frail.
Maybe this body knows something all on its own, about geology,
and about the healing in obscurity.

Layers; each a memory of the last remembered,
each changed "a hair's breadth" in resurrection.
Light glints off eyes, not as brightly.
Features move like cookie dough.
Wait, don't I know you?
A heart flutters.
Still?

October

A leaf tumbles down
from high in an oak
and with a last somersault
lands among its kin

Paving Stones

Paving stones slip past. Sandaled feet, leathery sounds,
the crunch of leaves underfoot.
I look across the yard and see across the years and miles.
There's Pop, his quilted jacket zippered up, rake in hand,
coaxing leaves into the flame.

I wait upon the smoke, the friendly smell of their burning.
And Pop, unshaved, lighting his stubby cigarette for the
umpteenth time.
Leaves and paving stones slip past, as does this moment's
recollection of short-lived contentment, that with all the
years and miles still brings half a smile.

The Familiar

Didn't we have an agreement?

Weren't you to be my mother?
Giving so freely.

I say this to the hills lined up against a pale sky.
I say, where is the warmth of that other, the one outside,
looking with such care and concern at the one inside.

My lips are tender, chapped,
feeling the dry wind that comes across the
fields at sundown.

Waiting

It's about to snow
A flake drifts down
Caught in the wind
is carried aloft again

"The Sum of the Facts…"

The things we get attached to: keep going back for another sip
from an empty mug.
"Sorry Henry, still empty, like it's been the last eighteen times
you lifted it."
Others are not really interested, not past the first couple
of words.
I don't hold that against them, it's too circular to merit much
attention.
Plus they have their own *tar babies* they can't keep their
hands off of.
Still, it takes a couple of years before you can find your
way again.
That's what it did me.
Oh, I was busy, schedules, commitments, agreements to fulfill.
And I did all that. Somehow got it done.
Busy also, sorting through the rummage sale of my mind.
It kept trying to take bits and pieces, of this and that,
and rebuild our house, the one that burnt down.

What did you do? What did you do?
Why?
My mantra. A lot of help.
Like the rest of us, you did what you had to, and probably,
in your own mind for sure, the best you could.

One part of my thinking trying to wrestle truth into focus.
Another trying to make it be you, sitting in the dining room,
looking up in an inquisitive, affectionate way, when I came in.
Creating tableaus of families that would never be.

Sorting it out, turning the clock so I can read its face.
I still pause crossing the threshold, but at least I'm in the
house, in the kitchen, buttering an English muffin.

What does that timepiece say? Do I want to know?
You'll tell me anyway.
It says, *The sum of the facts don't equal the truth.*

Ah, another smart-ass excited about discovering our solar system!

Heirlooms unlimited, museum pieces, dioramas of the Serengeti,
of sod homesteads, of our place, completely furnished including
family pictures and an aging ghost with an eating disorder,
seated at our dining room table.
Everything loaded onto a flatbed and hauled across this huge
country, till it all freezes in time.

Breaker, breaker, this is Able-One, do you copy?

Tunnel Vision

W-on-t some-one-h-e-l-p
-me!
yo-u dir-ty-f-u-c-k-e-r-s

It came to me recently, how we'd
watch the Mama-sans
dodge 50 caliber rounds. Anything
for a laugh.
chemical, biological ....

Meanwhile, Michaela is scared witless,
fearing *them* ... but gripped in obsession.
It's coast to coast!
She'll not be tempted into NY not even with
delicious promises: breakfast on 5th Avenue,
a horse drawn ride in the park
the ballet—she loves ballet.
Thirty-second broadcasts, on a loop, too much,
too astonishing—all gone, nine seconds.
But her mama cannot pry her off the couch
away from the TV, and its fraught, demonic unravelings.

I asked my good friend, "Steve. What's that smell hanging
in the air?"
All he said was, "You don't know?"

She sits, gathering more paralyzing imagery.
A twelve-year old expert on how to expect the worst,
and—the inevitable. Used to look at the towers from
the family's deck.
The sun glinting off them.

On the ward, a heavy woman, bound to a gurney, keeps up her
unrelenting pleas: … won-t some-on-e he-l-p-y-o-u-d-i-r-t-y ….
They manage her into a wheelchair, for a visit out of doors,
and someone's put a crocheted bonnet on her head; pretty pretty
bonnet atop a head filled with impotent and fathomless rage.
When you can't get around anymore, *I mean at all,* it's hard.
My father threw it in at that point. What would I do—
how about you?

Strapped to a gurney, in the corridor, watching the flow,
the passing of enemies and of those who can.
Yo-u di-rt-y-fu-c
a clean blanket with blue trim covers the works,
dark curls flow out from under that crocheted cap

A nurse calls, "If you see Mario, tell him to wait for me."

There's a certain comfort in that name, Mario;
though for some, any target will do.
Speaking of which, the other night, I went outside,
in all innocence to pee, and some little monster bit me on
the ankle.
Standing there, aiming in, bothering no one.
Stung, swelled, itched like hell. A local spider I suspect,
also out on business, waylaying strays.

"Coma stai?" Michaela's momma asks me.
"Tutto bene, and how are you?" I ask.
"I'm okay," she says, "I'm okay."
My ma used to say, *"I'm okay,"* like that, and I'd start
looking her over for bruises.

"How's the girl?" I ask.
"I'm worried." she says.

chemical, biological ...
"won-t-so-me-on-e---w-o-n-t-so-me-one?"

Notes and Coffee Stains

Merwin, Bukowski, Frost, Sharon Olds:
in the face of the skill of their stitching, I feel
awkward, heavy handed, a clod.
Going up against them, I'd shrink, like
an embarrassed penis—*is that all you got!?*—
if I let it get to me.

It is what it is—so I won't quit because of this,
this poverty of language, this ignorance of craft.
But I am not being feverishly attentive either.
It comes and it goes.

There's the old man, at 100 plus years, still calling
us to hang out, and let the layers slough off.
We gather. Finding resources,
trudging back to our place
in the sitting hall.

But one day, when the old man calls it quits,
a studio of daily life will be created. Piles
of papers and odds and ends will be set curbside.
Mail that has remained unread, will be, and my worktable
will once again be free of everything but notes and poems
and coffee stains.

Meantime this unfinished business calls—
this introspection,
and infers that all else can be addressed later.
After noisy worlds are silenced, or at least quieted.
After the crows, ravenous and very clever,
are given their due and move on.

After we quit stalling for time, and come
out of our corner, when the bell rings.

You Could Say That

J.B. said, "It's like the memory of a lovely fuck."
You could say that, and I have, being clouded, blunt,
drinking.
But it's not really like that is it?

More like, "a passing of fingers over …" or, "an intermingling,
your eyelashes with mine, green eyes searching green eyes,
bottomless …"
or the sound of rain on shingles,
where are you to hear this with me?
or yes,
yes it was.

One-Way Tickets

The thing I liked about you
was it was all about you
for me

I got to watch
witness
be an audience participant
What a welcome break to take
from the business of myself

Got to be a resource
helping out in that imperfect
life that flowed around a
seemingly perfect you

I knew better
but that didn't matter much
Your value added to mine
The usual struggle to gain traction
became a breeze

There were risks Yes
willingly eagerly taken
Deaf man walking the rails

Mr. know-nothing applauded
by his own in-house chorus
Seeing a thumbs up in every sun rise

Storms came
sink holes
the shake-up
lost traction of all kinds
They used to call it "the skids"

Ask Bettelheim that heroic model of
gauntlets run
an unspeakable raining of blows
then to somehow find one's knees
one's legs again
We can't ask, but he told us anyway

Her value added to his
his imperishable will enmeshed
along with that mystery of luck
What luck

One day we're faced with the truth
luck or no
This day's truth
Sometimes too big to face
of one-way tickets

Anyway—I got to watch
be an audience participant
help
And I liked that about you

Take Your Time, But Hurry Up

Overdue, I took a shower and caught my reflection
in the mirror.
Don't spend too much time grooming that body.

Careful not to break it, but don't fall in love.
We're not home yet, and the distance is
beyond measure.

Sidestepped

At times there's too much pain in words.
Lighten up.
Tell a different story.

On reflection, pain remains untouched.
Sidestepped, misdirected at every turn,
it lays coiled and virile,
waiting.

Aiming High

I no longer aim high.
Things get flirted with though.
Well, not really flirted, my self-esteem isn't that solid,
more like shooting craps with chickenshit bets.

Sounds funky right?
It's much better.
I've learned. For one, from my neighbor; his son barely talks to
him and won't let the grandchildren spend the afternoon anymore.

But he's good, so patient with his old hound. The dog is getting
more deaf all the time.
Like church bells in some antique Italian village, my neighbor
claps energetically, at the hours of vespers, to call the dog back
home.
Here's another good thing, the mutt is so old, he no longer climbs
the little hill to shit in my front yard.

Anyway, I've learned from my neighbor; where poor choices,
the law, and low income have made him keep it very simple.
A good natured guy, and there's no stink of resentment coming off
him, in spite of his difficulties

Aiming lower keeps me out of some real pickles, like having to
help save the planet, or anyone of personal significance—or
insignificance—on it.
How well did that work, way back when I knew so much?
When I knew what was supposed to be what.
I got frustrated, got mad, and got drunk.

A Dwelling Place

One said, "Yes."
The other said, "I can't say no to you."

What was it that broke the link and tainted his desire for her?
I thought it was her indifference,
now I'd bet the opposite was true.
She wanted more. There was no more.

And so—it came down to blood on the floor: incarceration,
banishment, crucifixion.
How mad she'd gotten, how righteous.
What they had between them, what had taken root, flourished
orchid-like in its subterranean existence, was not allowed.
Forbidden.
Verboten.
Nevertheless it grew, nurturing and molding them.

Taboos, they seem to make so much sense,
especially when they belong to your tribe.
A reasonable need, this imperative of restrictions,
given the bigger picture; time, continuity, and desire-mind's
predictable denial of inconvenient consequences.

Another thing, taboos contain such vitality, are such efficient
vehicles for our insatiable quest for oblivion, that they thrust
up and are lived out under the nose of Cotton Mather et al.
Denial prevails till the door bursts open.

A private world: caring, careful, nuanced, tender, and almost
completely blind.
Also, breathless, care-less, unquenchably lurid, inescapable.

An intimate terrarium.
Seemed perfect, but they didn't have a prayer.

The power of love, and its double-cross, is—you want to be who you love.
But if you're not careful, you'll wind up playing all the parts.

That said, she was angry, wanted potency, demanded it.

There was also a level of madness bleeding into all this.
She looked for allies and for outrage recognized.
Help me turn this indifferent tide.

The heart of things: that heart is warm, moist, and has room, lots of room for other hearts.
Absorbing, melding, becoming indistinguishable.
Sometimes circumstances funnel the flow, create purity,
even when the driver is oblique, twisted.
Purity is nondenominational. A kiss and the hunchback vanishes.

One said, "Yes." The other said, "I can't say no to you."
One said, "Yes." The other said, "Maybe hmm, yes—I'll never say a word." And the door of union closed without a sound.

But in our world, no door stays shut.
One said, "Yes." And one said, "Yes but shouldn't we ....?"
And one said, "Perhaps. Are you afraid?"
And got no answer.

Entwined again and again, grows a dwelling place—a home.
A front door, a driveway, a dining room table.
How to go on, in the face of no answer?
To be lost without losing it all?
If you can manage that, you might save yourself.

Beyond the smoke, the play for recognition,
what had wounded her most, she said in a quiet voice:
"He left to get his needs met elsewhere."

You wanted more. There is no more.

The Edge

Obliged to find our voice
to keep trying
Outside of reason beyond the constraints
where the thin air at the edge
and the thick muck at the bottom
are linked

Obliged to keep trying

A frog masked by grass and reeds
croaks at the water's edge
Obliged to find nothing

Dandelion Dreams

We didn't get far, did we, making dreams more than a
bird with clipped wings.
Trusting they would catch a breeze and sail.
But they were way too porous.

More porous than the downy spheres of dandelions.
Easily dispersed, absorbed in that space between molecules,
troubled by small disturbances, changes in barometric pressure,
a slight shift of emphasis.

Poor fellows we are, creating dreams to send out, hitchhike
across continents, score an internship, a fellowship,
create a monarchy.
Find their destiny, and ours, like some tangible asset.
Not likely; dreams are born with clipped wings, and us;
we are leashed, bound, and grounded,
praying for rescue.

Small Talk

In the year following our break up we spoke little
and never about us.
I kept my mouth shut, and waited for a hint,
a spark of interest.

Nothing.
Just small talk.

You only ever made two comments about us,
with a few months between each.

The first was: "If I could have believed you loved me,
I could have hung in."
What can one say? That's a hard nut to crack for a shot
at getting one's life back.

And the second nugget, the next important clue,
coming a few months later:
well—*I can't remember.*

Just Right

About now a nipple would be nice, just right.
Consider the consequences
Or an afternoon in the shade, gabbing with Peter,
in Roswell.

Sitting here in the front room, all the shades down except one,
is easy enough, no complaints.
Soon I'll get up, head cold and all, take a coffee and the
fern I've kept inside all winter, down to the porch.
Drink coffee in my tee shirt and pajamas.

Might get a visitor. Visitors show up now and then.
Lately with good vibes and want little.
Yesterday a neighbor borrowed the lawn mower and brought
it back ahead of time.
This morning though, an old friend called to say her house was
being lost, to a sheriff's sale.

"Could I help?"

Years ago I tried.
Pointed out: "Be careful, the hole is getting deeper,
and you're still digging."

Some of us, like children, love to dig.

Fred

Fred Henson passed over Christmas.

We went on spring break together, in his tidy green
Volkswagen Beetle.
Four of us, and our gear, a cozy fit.
Toby and her boyfriend John, Fred and myself.
Down to New Orleans from Chicago, for some fun and adventure.
Spring break over fifty years ago.
Seemed a fresh bright thing to do. Light, as in, not heavy.
On reflection, it still feels that way.

Bright, light, and the leaden skies on the horizon went
unrecognized.
I ate oysters for the first time. Toby too. We held out, in disgust,
for a couple of days, surrounded by crowds of oyster eaters.
Tons of oysters, tides of beer.
It was the beer that broke our will. I came away loving oysters,
raw with lemon and cocktail sauce—lovely. Still do.
And we had a nice time, even some serious excitement swimming in
the gulf, when the sharks swam up. Scared us near to death.
Amid a frenzy of splashing to escape, fear, and heroics
—John shielding Toby—the sharks magically turned to dolphins.

Fred has died, Toby will have heard. She'll be sad.

That woman was a true robust beauty in her time.
It's what I still see. She's got a couple of pictures on a dressing
table. *Ah, yes, there she is.*
Now she's cheerful with a tart wit, thin and a bit unsteady.
Though not as unsteady as Glen, her thinner little gentleman of
a husband.
Visiting, my thought was, *These two drink a lot to live in a*
house with so many stairs.

John and Toby did get married.
The "love of her life," she remarked.
Seems it didn't last. They were more successful courting.
Classic, in poor art-student mode.
John may have created a drinker's life. I won't go into it.
You want to know what that looks like, look around you.

So it's been a long time since I've heard of Fred, and now
I have again.
His neat little VW Beetle is out of this picture and he's gone west.

In between, an industrial design student, orderly, bright,
and reservedly congenial, created and lived out a life.

Probably a manageable tidy one. I'm filling in the blanks with
almost no info.
Fine—make it up for him.
Leave out the slander and the larceny, if there were any. Keep his
clean well-kept little VW in focus. Expand on that.

At the time I had a beat up VW Bus, which certainly set the pace
for my journey. No matter where it broke down, which was often,
I stopped, took out tools and ground cloth and went to work till
it was running again.

In bad weather (Chicago!), no joke. In winter–really?
Put out the tarp, get down, get under, work it—my life.

Fred's?
I'm sure he had Triple A.

He laughed, we can be sure of that. He was one of those low-key
planners that persevered and had his share of socialization.
A low-key but regular part of the group. He'd swim in the shallows.
Myself, I was more comfortable isolating, but tended to head for
the deep end when I showed up.

We were all too young then to screw it up too badly.
Misdemeanor level on the evolutionary scale.

Yes, we had lots of laughs and smiles and private worries.
More to enjoy than not.
And the promise made it almost breathtaking.
Some laughs were light, buoyant, floating by. Others in their joy,
were also attached to our soul, pulling on it as they drifted on.

Fred had a career, a steady job, found a wife (or she him),
had a child—hence some tears and fears among the laughter,
the cocktails and cigarettes.
Everyone I knew smoked. I wanted to, wanted to be like them,
but I'd turn green and get seasick.
Spread my wings and crash landed.

I broke up asbestos-laden boilers in old factories, he worked over
a drawing board, ate lunch at the appointed time, his regular tuna
salad or grilled cheese sandwich.
Followed his path, much of it I would guess, he was destined to
tread on, as was I mine.
Even had an occasional oyster, perhaps in New Orleans again?

I never returned till a few years ago.
Quaint, worn, tons of oysters, tides of beer.
I passed on them this time around.
It was good, Fred.
Still is.

A Touch of Defiance

She said, her green eyes sparkling with affection and
a touch of defiance, "I'm glad those other women treated
you so badly. It gave you the chance to find your
way to me."

I looked at her, this Irish child, trying so hard to be a
perfect grown-up, and she said before I could,
"I know, I know, I'm bad, but I'm happy you're here."

Meandering

A fine man, sensitive, considerate, though he got carried away.
"Tone it down" was suggested.
"Become a little disreputable and give yourself a break," was suggested.
He bit his lip, mulled it over, as much as he could,
and carried on.
Carried off he was, bobbing along, helpless as a leaf, but lacking the indifference.
"What's up? What's going on?" they asked.
"I'd be the last to know," his answer shouted from afar.

Lunchtime at the *Automat*. What I'd really like is chicken salad on rye.
My father, the one with the goods, the one with the magic powers, far surpassing the puny powers of other fathers, the one whose magic I will somehow one day make my own, to use, and win, win everything I need; he will give us nickels.
Small hands grasp priceless coins, and reconnaissance reveals such abundance, such delicious mysteries behind tiny glass doors.
Nickels tumble, little fingers hold miracles.

Smiles will become sparse when mysteries turn to secrets.
Carried away: bridges move past, the Triboro, I recognize the toll plaza from cab driver days.
Adrenalin days, spiced with eye contact, happy accident, semen splashes.
Ripples making ripples ...
See, she's moving up the hillside, jeans stretched over important hips, stretching again with each tilted step. She's heading west.
I am not.

Sorry, my direction has no compass point. An issue for the still ambitious. Very much so.
And I am still ambitious, though ignorant of the contradiction. Fortunately, they only go as far as the edge of our solar system; contradictions.
He glimpses an absorbent demeanor, an incoming smile.
Naïve,
energetic.
Isn't that about the same place we all started: smiles,
naïve,
energetic.

Our truth before the truth.
Encourages *meandering*.

E.R.

Well, you're at peace. I'm with you on that.
There were days though when we faced our situation
wanting to run like rabbits.
Of course, you'd have had to stop and light a smoke.
Still, I have no argument with stained fingers,
and the raw smell on smokers.
Necessary connections in the remorseless faceless first of all.

Recently I stumbled and the beast opened its maw.
Thanks to you, not my day to feed it.
You missed that, but I leaned your way.

Nevertheless, a bed with straps and rails may await me too.
What, did we trade up? At what cost?
Your nurse Mario, he helped.
We loved him for it, but he couldn't perform the miracle,
and started to cry with the rest of us.
Look, help me again will you—you're never out of reach—
to catch up, and not crash too early.

Pockets in my gut; they insist I give up significant small items.
More separation from the little pleasures.
Remember, facing our predicament, we found difficulty
in the trade off.
Like you, I wanted the juiciest parts.
Now they encourage—organ donation.
Hard to picture isn't it?
Then there's that urge to run,
like rabbits.

Walking Past

That man walking past can only
walk the truth
He had a stroke last year

A butterfly—it's said—can only
tell the truth

Sort that out in this
bouquet of lies we tell ourselves

Can a blank page be the truth
I begin and end with it

Bulgaria

Cereal with water—clam chowder sprinkled with cheerios
I'm out of crackers
The fridge is empty of everything but apples and
plum jam from Bulgaria

Going to have to go out of the house soon
There's a can of beef stew looking out of the cabinet
I'm saving it for hard times

Trackless

Across the lawn up behind that old spruce
a gray cloud fills the sky.

Then cloud and sky are lost in waves of thought.
Submerged in a cerebellum's trackless wanderings.

When I can see out again the big grey cloud is gone,
and a stream of smaller ones file past.
Clouds and sky filling every window and every open door.

A dragonfly darts up, seems about to crash,
then tests the glass with a nudge.

Down At Debs

At the water's edge
the pond rippled and deep green from
the rains
a heron steps out with long measured strides
The way he holds his head
you know
he's sure of everything

Yes My Dear

Let's take a look at Linda and Sam, her little gentleman husband.
Though it's Sam who is the main character here.
An intellectual, a competent provider, a success in his field.
And to his complete surprise, and some bewilderment
(*but I'll take it*), he wound up with "the best piece of ass on the planet."
Who me?

I've seen it happen a few times. Just last year—again.
Picture of the happy couple, the bride and groom, friends and family.
Or a social engagement, folks gathering for pictures.
She's always stunning, complete, stage center.
And he's like, "Let me pinch myself".
He feels like an unexpected guest, asked to be in the wedding picture by accident.
Who me?

I think of it as the Arthur Miller-Marilyn moment.

Here's how a story like this unfolds:
The stunning young (sometimes not so young) woman realizes, not for the first time, that her Edmund Hillary look-alike, after the initial robust locking of genders, has undesirable habits, childish behaviors. Less than meets the eye, so to speak.
It's getting old, wearing thin.
Their consolidation in security and reliability, their nest, is not happening, as attractive and well matched as they seem.

One day, walking home, she says, "Wait, did I just have a pleasant, intelligent conversation with that little guy in my yoga class? Can't keep his eyes off me, doesn't think I know."

Yes, it happens, and he's there for life. Easy to please,
impossible to really disappoint, happy most of the time.
And a real grown up when it comes to almost everything
else but "me."
Forever kind of dazed—amazed.
Even when she's ageing, unsteady, still telling him what to do
and when.

One old Irish fireman, with bad arthritis, was never more content
than to say, "Yes my dear," to his crabby high mileage beauty,
as he struggled to light her cigarette, while his loving niece could
only quietly watch, and cringe.

As Arthur might have said, gazing at *his* "best on the planet,"
it hurts so good, and I'm good with that.

The women are often a class act in themselves, nuanced,
intelligent, successful in much of the business of their lives.
Linda is brilliant and tasteful in the world of art and society.
Christine heads a team of medical consultants.
But then we all have our gaps, our sticky comfort zones,
where we can find ourselves a bit lopsided, a bit worn,
out of our depth.

Hey, no problem. *Let me pinch myself.*

Carefully

Bent low, Corporal Felkner and I, slowly, carefully cross a narrow
log over a wide stream.
At the first shots we spin and race back across that log,
as sure footed as monkeys.
Crouching, rifles brushing the grass, we keep moving,
and take immediate defensive action—
two tightly clenched ass holes.

The rising sun shining full in your face,
thoughts dancing madly behind closed eyes,
brightness creating star bursts, silhouettes.
Morning breaks opened.

On the other side of the day, slanted rays pierce the dense wood,
falling across a slope covered in pale green shoots.
Small stems with two or three new born leaves atop each one.
So eager, so many, erect in the setting sun.
And what is your destiny my tiny companions?

Oh, the Humanity

Some of my favorites have gone over the rail, just like that.
Or worse.

Can there be a worse or better?

Painful, sad, such beauty of spirit, of mind and the infinite possibilities in prehensile thumbs.
I've got to ask, why did you feel so compelled to do that?
Was it conviction or the lack of it?
Duality, that trap we must get clear of, driving us to one unfettered moment?
And was that duality flavored with being secretly pissed,
like bits of pecans in a bowl of Ben and Jerry's.

My birth father had some impressive disappointments,
losses, reversals, unfairnesses.
He took some beatings. It would seem, more than his share.
But he got through, or carried them with him, maybe wrapped up, boxed away.
Ended up sitting on the porch with his devoted cracker wife,
in his pj's, old slippers, and a trusting open smile.

My Pop, my other father, barely managed his miseries.
His hard-won treasures, degrading, eroding, except once in a while a brightness and generous sensitivity shone through.

The restlessness in both men, in their struggle against such personalized bondage.
Yet they never saw a dead-end here, even writhing in its periodic stink.
It's hard to figure, puzzling.

One feels a sadness that the sparse or dense beauty these others
purveyed got clipped.
Couldn't they lower their expectations,
be okay with what was left?
Stick around for it?
Some of us have such a hard time sticking around.

Is the unconditional that compelling?

Relief might come to us; onlookers, devotees, knowing why they
took a different course.
Or not having all this information, this identification.
This fascination: questions, ambitions, and our unwillingness to
allow them their choice.

They make us willing though.
How else could we touch their humanity?

It's just that some of us have a hard time sticking around.

Words

Words—they make me a person,
even in a room with no one for miles around,
and those that are don't know I exist.

And there's something to be said for that,
isn't there?

Worms

He called us worms.

You are not different than worms—mosquitoes.

I take offense!

(But how can we be sure?)

Seven Out of Ten

Here I sit early in the day.
The day's objects swirl around me.
Swirl fast, swirl slow.
Sitting in a bowl of warm milk, objects of desire float by.
Blueberries, raisins, bananas, crushed nuts—ouch!

Hurray, I can breathe underwater, my diaphragm finding a
rhythm that suits the consistency of an unctuous universe.
I can hear a dog barking, muffled and echoing off the inside of
the bowl of his world.

Well-aimed barbs flash towards me, but are caught-up,
snagged and miscarry,
mired in protective belts of viscous matter.

Like John Glenn, I never really got that far from home,
but it went right to my head.
I danced and clapped and bowed to the bleachers.
Joined the ornamental parade, even though consensus
claimed a near miss.

Ten out of ten would have been Senatorial.
I did get seven out of ten.
At five hundred yards—a long way out—seven bulls-eyes in a row,
before my personal history caught up, and I got the shakes.
So never experienced the public adoration that came with ten
out of ten.
I wasn't ready, the cook wanted me to taste the broth and get to
know the grunge of kitchens.
And the brittle side of beauty, what to make of it as it fractures.
How one breathes underwater and never loses sight of the shallows
and of childish ambitions.

It's all so brand new.
Let's swim the channel. Let's dive deep, really deep!

Ten out of ten would have been Presidential.
Tenure ensured.
It turned out okay, why make a fool of oneself outside the family.

FOUR

Thank You Sir

Thank You Sir

We were loved. That can happen. It did happen.
And it counts for more, in this scramble, than one has time
to recognize.
The scramble counts for little, even less, though we give it a lot
of credit, while doodling is disparaged, and whistling a lost art.

Those who loved us are now to be found where?
Not gone—not found.
I have nowhere to go, that's plain, and neither have they.
The hard part is I can no longer think of them in the usual ways.
We used to share a sandwich, you'd make pasta on Fridays.
I'd button the back of your dress.
You'd say, "Thank you, sir."

Thinking like that, following its causal path, bears fruit with a sad,
bittersweet taste.
Soils the time when we looked out the same portal, anticipated
arrivals and departures.
From her bed, his wife told their children, almost grown, "Your
dad will find a nice lady, after this. He has such good taste."
And he did. And they are good together, and blessed by whom?
How could she now wish those two a life beset by lumps
and furrows?

Shouldn't we learn to leave our loved and lovers as they are?
They no longer wear the clothes we would dress them in.
Loosen your belt, let your shirt hang out, sit on the porch in
your slippers. Stop talking.
You say, "They are not here. They are not here!"
If we are, they are.

Seeing that is so easy, we are blind to it.
Checking, examining, making it up.
Shadows and guises, leaving no stone unturned,
no speculation uninvestigated.
Testing it all in the heat of purpose.
Nothing itself doesn't work for us.
Everything works for them.

If they are, we are.

Once Upon a Time

Somewhere, in a church, a cathedral, a museum,
I saw this stone coffin from the Middle Ages.
About the size of a big bed.
The thick stone lid had the full figures of a noble couple
sculpted into it.
Fine stonework, they looked so lifelike, lying next to each other,
dressed for a special occasion.

I see her clearly, an attractive young woman with long hair
close to a nicely shaped head, tresses over her shoulder, a delicate
stone face.
A long gown to her ankles.
And small feet.
Her gown was open at the neck and she wore a large ornate
necklace.
Around her waist, one of those fascinating Middle Ages belts,
heavy, following the curve of her hips,
the rise of her lower belly.

Next to her, her husband, bigger, and overdressed,
vests, weapons and pointy boots.
As I remember, he wore a sort of pleated stone skirt over
his leggings.

The tableau was—pensive.

At the time I thought, skilled and meticulous.
But for what?
It's all just stone,
the reality is inside the coffin.

Then I noticed, they were holding each other's hands,
palm to palm, fingers entwined,
your pulse and mine.

Afternoon to Evening

Blue grey sky fills my afternoon.
A mountain ridge cuts rough diagonals across it.
The mountain blanketed in reddish browns and greens.
The sky, unblemished.
One empty, the other massive.

The pond out front gives its rippled confirmation.

Afternoon to evening.
Bats crisscross the transition.
As the sky darkens, mountain and ridge line start to swallow their own detail.
All the places of interest, the nooks and crannies, merge into indistinct shades of grey and shadow.

Evening,
and a once weightless sky is gaining substance. Its darkening geometry leaching matter from everything around it, while the thick mass of the mountain is feeding itself to the night.

In the dark,
surfaces are covered in a sheen of moonlight.
Pond and night reflect a brilliant sky—an endless living presence.
And the mountain: just a whisper.

Confluence

In dreams a beauty resides unchanged
leaking excitement into the night's quiet
Sweet water deep harbors schools of bluegills
flashing by
Gardens mango trees tropi-*cahl*

a surge of pubes moves past
screened by the foliage
a dizzying prospect

He said, "Shake hands my friend."
A chance we take not eagerly smiling with knotted guts
Those hands
where have they been these last tumbled decades

hair fingers tongues flapping
lips parched cracked should they be kissed
and they may
they will
will love be birthed

Fruit trees first shoots schools of bluegills flash past
ever reflective of especially toxicity
We find ourselves moving amongst them
chirping our songs of joy of mindless bliss
or mindless apprehension

Moist and humid beneath mossy mantles
drops sticky sweet nurture parched lips
on occasion cool air wafts through
heady
a confluence of promised peace and almost—
dreamless sleep

Embers

I looked at the mother and
saw in her her daughter
I looked at the daughter and
saw in her her father
I looked at the mother and
saw in her a lover
from another time

Longing—palpable
the way her weight shifted at
the hips when she laughed
the light in her broad smile

Did she not sense it
our connection
damped back to a faint glow
living still

I looked at the daughter and
saw in her the future—holding
a poem in which the second hand
and the minute hand stop
illuminated by embers

Awakening

Pale, lithe, she stood before me.
Her heart soft.
So soft, she might slip away unnoticed,
like the shyest of children.
Shy, quiet, about to slip away, except
for curiosity, except for appetite awakening.
It guides a small hand to reach, to touch.
Causes her face and eyes to open in a smile,
a smile that goes back to a time, even before Leda.
Before deities and mortal selves went their
separate ways.
Before craving or indifference created wings and
quests, and miracles,
and small feet running.

Closer to the Bone

Kitchen Cat lies waiting.
A bird feeder sways in the early morning breeze.
Birds who refuge for the night in cottonwoods
nearby come to perch and peck—or pick from spillage
on the ground.

Black and white, she bounds, blurs across the sidewalk
jumping among the birds and seeds!
Mountain jays and finches leap into the air, chattering,
scolding a too slow cat.

Too slow, too fat, its prowess dulled by kitchen fare
and sunshine.
Beware you mountain jays and chatty finches,
another cat may cross this yard
with fur less sleek and skin much closer to the bone.

Idyllic

It's a perfect summer day.
Sun and clouds and a slight breeze pass over
the hills.
Idyllic, walking the shaded paths.
I even came upon a clearing of wild blueberries.
Who could resist.
A handful of late summer blueberries, deep misty blue,
firm, and ripe.
Munching and strolling along.

Too bad about the *runs* I got later. Whew!
Serious!
It must have been those little pits in the berries,
nice and chewy at the time.

Otherwise, *idyllic*.

Day After Day

Standing on the bank, looking down at the creek's unhurried
passage.
But I hardly see it.
What I see is a car in need of a new bumper and maybe
a timing belt.
And houses with "For Sale" signs on them.
One says, "Under Contract."
I see chubby girls that run my lawyer's office with fierce,
streetwise efficiency.
One of the girls walks by in a dress a bit tight for her soft,
ever-increasing bottom, which jiggles.
Is that the effect she wants?
I wouldn't, but girls in their mid-thirties may see things
differently, have goals that will ever and gratefully remain
a mystery to me.

Ah, there, through the leaves and branches, the morning sun
ricochets off the water.
It happens day after day, decade after decade, and they never
miss their appointment, or wear each other out.
Obscured again by rush hour's invasion.
Horns, traffic jams, people in a sweat.
And there's Rosa, clients on hold, papers to attend to,
a typed page waving in her hand as she talks and smiles at me.

Soon she's telling me about her kids, her son who is adorable.
"See here's his First Communion picture, but even that young,
he's already like his know-it-all dad."
Listening, I give myself up to it.
Rush hour passes endlessly. You can fight it out, or sit it out,
as it inches towards its countless destinations.

A mosquito dives into my ear, and the woods and stream reappear sharp and clear.

A walking stick that someone left leans against a rock.
A book never read, but was asked to in a kindly way,
comes to mind.
Add it to that assortment of small omissions that change the course of events. Omissions, additions, subtractions:
History.
It jiggles.

Metronome

Dancing on the inside of a baroque tapestry.
Untroubled.

Dancing among the gold, the red, the green threads.
Being enveloped completely in the sound of the metronome.

Then I noticed, in a gray blazer and dark slacks,
the dance-master.

The Visitor

Before heading to the hospital
where Janis is dying
I pay close attention to washing
up after breakfast.

A bowl, a butter knife, and especially
an old spoon I've had forever.
Cleaning and smoothing its surface, rinsing off the soapy
bubbles.
Watching them pass through my fingers.

Not Allowed

I could tell he wasn't going to amount to anything
even when he was a baby. A toddler.
Quietly watching us from the far side of his comforter,
with the hint of a miniature smile.

Maybe it was passed down from his mom.
She was also into be-ing. A beautiful radiant be-ing.
Since just be-ing, long term, is frowned upon,
and a commitment to it not allowed,
be-ings are charlatans. They come up with ruse after ruse
that put inquiring minds to rest.

With that they can just be; could-be-forever.
Buddha's an example, because he wound up—simply
thoroughly—indistinguishable.
But didn't he work up quite a sweat
getting to that drop point?

Indeed, perhaps passed down from his mom.
She stayed in college for almost a lifetime.
What better place for just decently, humanely abiding.
On leaving, she encountered such brashness,
such ambition, such innuendo, that she went back to the Halls.

Now, decades later, he gently navigates the ant colony.
Finding respite, announcing, in his undemonstrative way,
a truly interesting prospect.
Even producing deceptively genuine flurries of activity.
But I see him watching us, a hint of a smile on one side of his
mouth, letting the chain of events unfold.
I know already, it's hopeless, all is lost.
And how can you not love him for that?

Gripped in a Tight Fist

Time passes, comes back, passes,
is cooked up, recreated, held onto, and recycled.
Gripped in a tight fist, wrestled with,
surgically intervened upon, fattened up,
and trimmed.
Accepted and surrendered to.

Is it ever true?

Pirouette

In fourth grade I developed a twitch.
It involved my right eye and right cheek.

One day, a friend, David Sanuto—who lived in a nice house with
a well-kept yard, and a paved driveway—his father was a tile man.
We looked up to David, he was clear about things, assertive,
a leader, and had a successful Dad.
One day he said: "Gary, you've got to stop that twitch."
I responded emphatically, "I know!"

I did know, cause I struggled mightily with it every day.
And the next day always started with my resolve to do a
better job.
Control, that was my goal—control it—you can't just stop
twitching.
I'd already lost that battle, so the plan was to only twitch when
no one could see.
Sense it coming, hold it back, turn away, walk away,
let it twitch—twitch in secret.
Then be with friends again till the next spasm's approach.

It hardly ever worked.
"Darn! My twitch just went off and they saw it!"
Pause, regroup, "Come-on Gar, do better—you've got to."

Nevertheless, David Sanuto is the only living soul that spoke a
word of it out loud. He had his say, energetically, but that was it.
No one else.
Not my teacher, not my sister, or other friends,
not my mother or father.

I imagine my folks spoke of it between themselves:
"Gerri, you notice the boy's got a twitch. He tries to hide it.
He's too young to be jerking-off, so that's not it."
"Oh Dan, I see him struggling. A nervous tic. Please don't say anything. He can't help it."
"Okay, no, of course not. I just hope he's not turning out to be a defective."

Eventually—by fifth grade, it morphed from my face to my right hand and wrist.
An involuntary twist and pirouette of wrist and hand.
A blessing. Easier to hide, blend into other moves, or make believe you're doing it on purpose.

Blending, you can't beat that, and sometimes you catch a break.

Tears and Drinks All Around

You know you can't keep all this

Be still and things start to slough off
icicles melting from the eaves
a bloated mosquito lands on its back
unable to fly—encumbrances falling away

Sit still—a porousness of thought and phenomena
take over—a rightness in the body,
knots and twists melding
spines finding their proper attitude

Sit still—and boundaries overlap
silently fuse become
continuous indistinguishable

until
no longer sitting no longer
alone no longer

Wait—you mean dead?

Oh no—don't give me dead
As soon as you find me dead you and anyone
involved starts heaping it on
Expectations regrets history
tears and drinks all around
All the crap it took all this work to unload

Followed by
a parade of ghosts carrying more
junk then the living

Let's start again, just sit, mouth shut, in neutral gear
allow yourself to be your own masterpiece
and
a rummage sale

Just In Case

I went in and sat on the can.
I had to go, and also I had to blow my nose.
But first, there were preparations to make.
I neatly folded some lengths of toilet paper,
and set them, ready for use, within easy reach.
Just in case.

Just in case, one of the boarders in my parents' big old rooming
house, had to use the bathroom.
I'd hear him walking down the hall, footsteps distinct on
the linoleum.
Then he'd come up—*Oh No!*—and try to open the bathroom door.
Jiggle the handle.
Before he reached the door, I'd start making "someone's in here!"
sounds.
Coughing, throat clearing, foot tapping.
Discomfort and rage would stir in my 9-year old bowels.
"I'll be right out," I'd holler through clenched lips.
There would be a grunt or some acknowledgement from the other
side, as the boarder let go the knob and walked away.

Just in case, I heard my father yelling about something,
or someone, or, god-forbid, me.

A few minutes ago, like right now, October 7th, in my own home
with the white porch, the big yard spotted with evergreens, I still
found great comfort in the blank bathroom door between me, and all
that, all them.
Prepared in the customary way, *just in case*, I reached for a tissue
and finally blew my nose.

One day, in Enlightenment, I'll be able to shit in peace,
and blow my nose when it starts running.

Yoshin's Forest

Under a canopy of beech and maple we gather
shifting in the gusts and flurries
slowly changing with autumn

And in each of us a place bracing itself
for winter's muffling blanket

Unclaimed Baggage

It came down to
the brick and mortar of my life
weightless and transparent

Decks Awash

Seams bulge and split, rivets pop like buttons.
A green mass pours in, to smother and claim.
This will-less giant is sinking, decks awash,
going down, down deep.

Choking caught, even so giving way.
Holding on, unyielding, yet relief calls.
There is a sweetness somewhere.
The water, with a chill warning, starts to pull life out
through calves and thighs.
One's will begins to move with the enormity of events,
becoming microscopic, subatomic, a cloud of stars in infinity.

Out of blackness, into blackness,
from the deep I surface
to bob upon the swells,
and slick with oil, survive.

Cough, spit, restart the journey, washing and washing at the
oily stains of reclamation.

We'll Catch Them

Walking home from classes
It's fall and already cold in Chicago
Up ahead a fire—a family on the roof
five flights up

Firemen begging, yelling into their bullhorns,
"Throw down the kids! Give them a chance!
Throw us the kids!"
A huge round canvas net firemen holding
all around
waiting hoping guts in a knot

"We'll catch them
they'll be ok
Save them!
Throw us the children!!"

How does a mother throw her two little
ones into the night from up there
peering over crying yelling
alone
She couldn't take the chance

What would I have done

On the sidewalk far below I knew
A crowd of us did—gasping shouting encouragement
throwing our conviction and all the persuasion
our hearts could muster
Up-to-them

Up there choking—paralyzed—who can say
Outlined in the smoke and searchlights
Three—nowhere to run

Lives whole lives coming and going
playing out their brief journey
just like that

It's fall—already cold on Chicago's north side
walking home from classes—step after step
on a brief journey of my own
I thought I knew the way

Harvest Moon

Darkness—a series of closings.

You left, but not in darkness; in light, in life, the open road,
that open wound.
Darkness is shuttered, concluding.
At least from this side, the side we get dressed on; brushing
our teeth, looking in the mirror at someone looking back.
We know that person, hair growing wildly, and don't we own that
finger pressing the switch on the coffee pot.

Darkness is in a hurry, rapido. Shutting down the day with the
steady hand of complete indifference.
After a bit, we find the day again, dressed in a carpet of grass.
Thick and comfortable to the touch.
Alive in that sensation, or looking into a stream with a sandy
bottom, watching pebbles move with the current, watching
ashes from someone's cigarette float downstream.

Left for the open road—so it seems.
Its vistas, its promise.

Left on the open road. That holds a different kind of promise.
A wellspring of difficult possibilities.

Years ago, you could thumb a ride.
Nowadays people have too much information.
They already know the worst of you and pass on by.
Before you can explain, you're tagged, and bandaged.

Slow to heal, easy to pick at. With time a weeping wound.
Harvest moon, lovers June, weeping wound.
Many can't, many won't, but it heals if you let it.

Harvest moon, lovers June.

Ground

Body-mind always sings the same song:
Mother, come with your strokes, your caresses,
your murmurs.
Make me happy again.

I see her; there are tears in her eyes.
She knows what I don't want to see.

Side By Side

We sat in the car, side by side,
two lumps.
She had make-up on, and a dark suit,
her brown hair longer.
Me: baggy, non-descript, slouched.
She cried a little, and kept her composure,
almost.
I cried a lot, was swamped in it and blubbering,
more or less.

At some point I murmured, "What about our beautiful love?"
Like it was something not us; created by us,
nurtured, cherished, bigger than us.
Yet had somehow, incomprehensibly, been set aside,
left behind, withered.

That we had become indifferent, though I knew that could
not be true.
Indifferent to the blood in our veins,
the heavens?
How can that be?

It is said, "There is nothing deader than the dead."
And some of us shuffle on more easily than others.

Vespers

Outside black night and bright stars look down
with crisp familiarity
Frost descends

From deep within the darkness eternal warmth
rises coats the galaxy in dew

A rough wooden floor presses my bare feet
we meet as friends

Fingers beckon
tender and familiar

Like a toddler I move from uncle to cousin
from treasure to treasure

Wildflowers

We were wildflowers
you and I

Became a wreath of chrysanthemums

We are wildflowers
you and I

For Barbara and Mike Mulcahy

That's Easy

I see your name on my holiday list, tucked in
with friends and acquaintances.
Why are you on this long list of people
I want to send a greeting to?

That's easy—it's affection.
Love bridging a river of years.

For Carol

Sisters

Two sisters, visiting.
I look into the face and eyes of one, a familiar, warm connection.
Behind those soft brown eyes, the freshness of little girl business.
Youth seeking recognition, approval, lively responses.

With the other, slightly askew: grey-green eyes, like a sled dog,
a husky.
Behind them an untamed mindscape: Northland, pines and ice and
campfires.
And from there she looks into me, curious and searching, perhaps
for my home, the real one.
What's it like, and is she welcome there?

Not able to help myself, I scoop her up, hold her close, speak in a
soothing voice, carry her to safety.
Warmth and safety, if only for a moment.
She knows, molds into my chest a small body that I must soon set
down and give back to the wilderness. She does not fear it; home.

I let it go, let her go, I have to. Yet she is with me.
I know those eyes, looking behind mine, and the campfires.

Fire Sale

I.
"You should know," she said, "you did nothing wrong.
It wasn't you."

And I do know, for who else remains?

A fire sale, a going-out-of-business sale.
Love left early.
The crowds came later, rushing in from all directions.

By day's end there were just some torn boxes,
and a few shopping bags of odds and ends.

II.
Like the old neighborhood in the Bronx,
I dream myself back every once in a while,
and then let dreams spawn dreams.

Dreams competing with dreams, good ones
outrunning bad ones, or the reverse.
But they can't stand against the heat rising off asphalt streets,
or kids tearing through a crowded sidewalk on their bikes.

When you look around, see a day rolling itself out
in front of you, there's a yearning to step into it,
and a yearning to go back inside.

Your Name?
"...macht frei"

She asked, "What's your name?"
I said, *No name.*
She said, "Look at me."
No eyes.
She said, "Touch my hand."
Hands reach, no fingers find...

The sound I never welcome is back.
Ah, now that I listen carefully, it's gone.
That sound, a sound too full of despair to
bear scrutiny.

I ask her, *Are you my mother?*
"Too late for that!"
My lover, my solace?
"Keep dreaming!"
A slightly rounded belly, breathing.
Attend the rise and fall.
Another sound with no beginning.

Then she said, "It's over. You are now free: to laugh, or cry, or just leave it alone."

She asks, "Which will it be?"

No lips, no mouth, no...
The sound I never welcome,
it's coming.

Revved

Thinking of you
brightens me

FIVE

The Mole Penthouse

An Easy Way Out

Every day a little more
every day a little less
This tussle that ebbs and flows

For a guy sold early on
on miracles
it's hard to give up
an easy way out

Boundaries

I looked over to tell the time
and found that it was telling me
of schedules of how I was doing and
what I was doing
Telling me of boundaries recognized
goals met or lagging of bills due and
vacations done and
how was it going…
Better but not as good as it could
and ever so quietly in quiet
persistence reminding me
that so much still awaited

From a fabled mountain's edge I looked
down at the city
A valley of glowing flickering lights
houses boulevards
Criss-crossing it all like the second minute
and hour hands of a clock
ribbons of red-taillights winding
and blinking in streams of purpose and ambition
fused into molten rivers of heads and tails

Inside under a roof so many roofs
the kid next door who's still crying
Mom's soothing tone comes and goes
families kids restless neighborhoods
A mutt that won't stop barking
Purposeful ribbons so much so individual
meaning is soaked up in the ebb and flow
in the choke of time

In my gut a longing
Is it to get back onto that porch
into our yard
a gate to swing on
Is this wading against the tides and the
ribbons of light that ride them
going anywhere
The roar of surf too distant to be heard—but felt
Do I get it yet—the futility of snatching that brass ring

Making It Up

I stepped off the path to look at a pile of boulders,
stacked by bygone giants,
and the purple Manzanita trees.
Coming back, my cuffs, my socks had tiny burrs
all over them.

Simple—flawless.

Is there more?
You might say yes, of course there's more.
In your conviction and perhaps your honesty,
I might believe you.

Pulling it off, a burr bites into my fingertip.

Mountain Bird

Cedars cling
boulders lie embedded

Mountain bird plummets
through sun and shadow

A distant noise

Morning Zen

The hard wooden knock of the Han
softens
in falling snow

For Xiaoqing Zhu

Staying in the Game

He was an excellent storyteller, telling stories in the dark.
But that didn't crack the nut, nor rend the knot.
And it will crack, or unravel, when it's ready, though you
can't tell when.
A clap of thunder, descending at just the right moment?

One gets worn, but not worn out.
And enthusiasm wanes, ok too.
And then there is the scudding, the apparent wandering and drift,
like a skiff out on a blustery sound.
His hand, white knuckling the tiller, the other hanging onto the
brim of a windblown hat.

A boy, mute, wheelchair bound, sits in the dark, listening.
He hears everything, every intonation—the story surges in
his brain.
The colors, the dialogues.
He already knows the knot cannot be untied.
It will take a blade, and a clap of thunder.
And he will wield the blade

Oil Found on the Moon

I'm a lucky one, I see. That outer layer, its folds,
its patterns.
Not that that will answer.
Something's not perfectly all right in the dream world.
Love, almost complete, but not.

A four-day beard, no problem. My back hurts, I don't care.
Eating cereal three times a day; ok.
The struggle is—slipping in and then—coming out. Once inside,
no problem.

Serious?

Seems so.

Being sure might be worse.

Where is this love, this promise that does not evaporate
so readily?
Some of you know what I mean, even if you can't put it into
words either.
That dreamy dream world, a door you open and close—the
muffled clink.

And oh, you mentioned kids, thank goodness for them.
Those we can't abandon, can we? Our tether to the day.
Dawn finds us bent almost double, walking fast. Keep up, keep up,
don't cave. Keeping up; so hard.
For those who can't, once inside, no problem.

Unknowable

In the woods at 4:00 a.m., meditating.
It's arid here, the trees, park-like, with little undergrowth.
Wild oak, Manzanita, and a vibrant night sky.
I look at it for a spell.

These last nights, two shooting stars.
Meteorites that enter high above, to live in a bright brief pass across our world.
This morning I saw a third, streaking from unknown to unknowable.

In a couple days I'll shave, pack up and leave here, to visit a friend I haven't seen in 45 yrs.

For Dale Erickson

Think About It

At the table, if you gnaw on bones you will be called out, especially chicken bones.
Cats will whine in envy and the cook, hearing your disturbing crunch, crunch, may pick up a large wooden spoon and stalk towards you on short, determined legs.

If you must be primitive, do it with your back turned
and hunched, or better, alone in an alcove in the pantry.
You'll get more joy in there, gnawing on whatever part of the victim you choose to.

Gnaw discreetly though, or loved ones will leave the table, and desserts may go unserved.

Think about it.

Budapest

Have I forgotten what it was like to be broke?
Maybe.
Every time I reach into my pocket there's money.
Every time I need a thing I reach in there or write a check.

Feels like it's always been that way, available.

Curious, when we're full, we all but forget what it's like
to be hungry. That knot in my gut, the sometimes dull,
sometimes sharp ache of worry about how things are
going to play out.

Looking out the window, glancing at the new porch roof.
Nice, but it was expensive.
I don't quite know how I managed it.
It wasn't magic, but there it is.

Chocolate Bar Love

From Eva, my bookkeeper's Girl Scout sale, chocolate bars.
No, wait, she has three boys.
From her boy's catholic school chocolate bar sale.
Delicious.
I bought ten dollars' worth, and told her to give half away.
I'd just eat them.

I already pay thousands to my little Italian dentist.
We have interesting conversations, about Omega-3's,
the benefits of soymilk, and big fair-skinned Brazilian girls,
half his age, and eager for things.
He loves them.
Tall, full ... where to begin?! But, good for him.

The five chocolate bars that Eva dropped off,
eaten in two days.
Bad but transporting.
As a lifelong procrastinator no longer drinking, chocolate
bars are a wonderful means for delaying the inevitable.

Heartburned

Like some slovenly caricature of trailer park love,
she yawned into the phone,
on our phone call.
The better part of the day I'd lived in the hope
that this call would—move me up!

A yawn pricked distinct holes in that fantasy.
Air, hot, not unlike a yawn-in-reverse, emptied into the ether.
The same ether that fishing with no bites and failed
trifectas inhabit.

Got to laugh at how far the slightest whiff will take us.
Talk about fuel-efficient high mileage.
Of course, there's that after-burn.
Ever cross the street behind an old 2nd Avenue bus?

You got to be impressed though, the raw talent,
the agility of this…, this person, to deconstruct
one's most promising adolescent playbook, with a yawn.

I'm done.

Coho

Mik said, "The salmon run has started. It's supposed to be good this year.
We should go catch some."
"Sounds like a plan." I said.
So he called up a friend, who was big on fishing, to see if we could borrow some gear.
"Sure buddy," the friend said. "I'll meet you guys in an hour down at the cove."
An hour later, overlooking the sound, our fisherman set us up with poles, tackle and rigs.

"You guys are familiar with all this right?" he said.
"Nope," Mik replied. "Hardly ever fished, in all these years on the island."
I said, "I'm from back East visiting. Usually use worms, catch carp and sunfish in Franklin Pond."
"Really?" was all he said. Then added, "Okay, okay, it couldn't be easier." And he showed us.
He just cast out a line, and bam! Got a hit and pulled in a salmon. Not huge, but big enough for us to be impressed.
Five or six pounds in about two seconds!
"See, no problem."
"Wow," was about all one could say, and we started to get excited.

"See you tomorrow, I'll pick up my gear. Have fun."
And he left us on the curved shore of the sound, smacking our lips, raring to go.
There was a line of other fishermen, on either side, about every 50 feet or so, fishing away, pulling them in.
We started casting our lines along with the rest. Casting and reeling, casting and reeling.

Meantime, the chunky couple to our right, they looked kind of down at the heels, were literally filling up their beat-up station wagon with salmon. Both of them, just reeling them in.
We watched close, imitated their every gesture, and kept casting. But we did not catch any fish, not one big juicy salmon took our hook.

After two hours we had one out of the four original poles left in usable condition.
The rest were stripped, tangled, or incomprehensible.
Mik, lips compressed, teeth set, said, "I'm done, I give up. We can't get it right!"
I kept at it another half an hour and then we, flummoxed, frustrated, and full of envy, called the whole thing off.

It was as if we were in some unsuspected agreement, some mystical harmony, with the Coho, so they could swim past us unmolested.

We drove back to Mik's perfect cedar house, in his perfect cedar and mushroom forest in quiet disappointment. It was sad.
Sydney was in the kitchen and gave us a cheerful hello.
"The fishermen return home from the sea. How'd it go?"

"Mumble, mumble," and we handed over our lone salmon, caught not even by us, *in about two seconds*, and "mumble, mumble," we slumped into chairs at the kitchen table.
Sydney, the true treasure on Puget Sound, cried, "Oh wow! What a big beautiful salmon. More than we can eat. We'll grill it."

And that we did, and had a delicious, happy dinner on the cedar deck.
Grilled salmon, corn on the cob, sliced cucumbers and tomatoes,

all from the garden, and lots of bread and butter.
Mik and Sydney even had a celebratory glass of wine.

But let me tell you what upsets me.
It's not the fricken' salmon that outsmarted us all afternoon.
What upsets me is that chubby rundown couple fishing next to us,
filling that rundown station wagon of theirs with fish.
Big ones, little ones (there weren't really any little ones),
more than they could ever eat!

And us?

Autumn Upon Them

A shawl over chilled legs
autumn upon them

But bare headed and clearer
than spring

And It Was True

After the detonation that dissolved my ordinary life,
I went to an old Zen Master, soaked in wonder and apprehension.

He said: *Listen.*
And I listened.

He said: *Become–nothing itself.*

What's more ordinary than that?
And I found I was, and had always been, *nothing itself.*

A young Zen Master said: *Stop.*
And I stopped.

Peter, a friend from way back, said:
*If you're that ignorant, accept the consequences
and start learning something.*
Whoa!

Carol, my treasure, said: *I love you.*
And it was true.

Very Early

Walking on a mountainside, blanketed in
streaming snow.
My face, my eyes, my whole body tasting it.

The storm, grey, white, lit from within,
a mountain wall rising,
becoming part of wind and weather.

Clear against the brightness, a flight of blackbirds,
darting, swooping,
punctuation by the handful, thrown into the coming day.

Black Robes

Striking the Inkin bell to start Zazen.
It rang clear and pure.

Back on the altar, the bell tumbled,
clattered to the floor, and rang
clear and pure.

Runaway

The Blackshirts came, destroyed their shop,
their voice,
murdered his brother.
He was out
and lived.

Voices for a better future—the indifference of death.

He ran.

Bittersweet

Can't just be me, you must be part of this.
You are.
The light, the light that calls my heart to open.

Fields, the breeze, this dusty road comes to life.
Joy, tears of joy,
and the sadness we all carry.

How interesting it all is,
especially your every movement,
especially the scent of your hair.

Two worlds become one,
one world disappears
in a smile.

I miss you already.

Love Prevailed

A blond lady, well groomed,
fed her fingers into a teacup terrier's muzzle.
Its wet nose and tongue—transporting her.

An Indian couple, with the same profiles,
looking through each other's thick glasses into big dark eyes
enjoying the delights.

Encouraged to begin boarding the plane, a large lady
continued to sink her teeth into another piece
of deep-fried chicken.

My daughter said, as a little one, "Dad, I'm glad you didn't
get killed in the war. Because if you did, I wouldn't be me,
I'd be somebody else."

Love prevailed.

In Their Reflection

I started crying, crying for Mimi.
Inside I knew, she's fine now, I'm crying for myself.
Soothing it is. Selfish at a glance, but really just soothing,
ending better than it began.

Settled in respiration, humid, warm,
rising to coat the heavens in tears.
Tears, streams into rivers of them, return home.
In their reflection, a star for you, and a quarter moon for me.

The Bluff

Rolling over the bluff
clouds, brilliant under the midday sun,
paint a field of boulders.

Your Face

I saw your face

the light falling around it

and thought you were still here

A Garden

Dear Lord protect lovers like us
for we are blind and defenseless in this
complete surrender

A garden without carnivores
by your grace
Teeth, talons, the panther's growl
clothed in this special peace
tenderness

a story

The Mole Penthouse

Pop was born in Geneva, Switzerland in 1900. I can't help but think of that time in history, turn of the century till after the First World War, as a time of everyday heartbreak. Hey, we have them now. I've had some humdingers, but they are the exceptions, not the rule.

What does that do to people, create in them?

You listen to the family stories, the lost kids, the wife you loved beyond words, goes to the hospital to birth a child, and no one comes home, a small cut and it eats up a life, or, on the wrong side of politics gets you murdered. A commonality of everyday powerlessness over every day's content.

Let's face it—this author lives in a fat world with fat expectations. We are among the few that do. I admit though, listening to these stories, reading of the journeys, even like Hemingway's "For whom the Bell Tolls," created an adolescent knot, a sadness, in me that was never far away.

Paraphrasing H. Coben: Yes, *death is a great teacher; it's just too harsh.*

Pop was the youngest of five children ... four boys and a girl named *Anna*. Anna died early on, of one of those illnesses that took so many children. The boys were *Bruno, Elysé, Valerio,* and *Donato*. Pop was Donato, which became *Daniel* when he jumped ship and stayed in the US—or America, as he called it. "New York is America; the rest is just the United States."

The family lived in Geneva. His father had a tailor shop on the second floor, above street level. Back then, a shop on the second floor was a sign of class.

Pop said they lived pretty well when he was very young, but his father had severe sinus issues; he had an operation to get some relief.

The operation was a failure, as were many in those days, and it left him blind. A blind tailor. You can feel that one.

He therefore faded and died.

Pop said he could follow their descent into poverty, a mother and four sons, even with Bruno and Elysé, the eldest brothers, scraping up whatever work they could ... because the poorer you were the farther you were from water.

In their heyday, with his dad's tailoring business, they had a cold water tap in their kitchen. (Regular folks never had hot water taps).

After the family losses, he remembers water at the end of the hall, then water in the courtyard, until it was them on the upper floors of a tenement, and the communal fountain a block away in the square.

Bruno, as the eldest son, took over managing the boys, keeping them in line, as in herding cats. His model for discipline was the typical central European model of that time, heavy handed; you got your lumps. Apparently, Pop, who was gutsy and curious, got his share.

Being on the receiving end of that kind of treatment can put a mean streak in a person. It did me.

But then, a mean streak may be what it takes to keep getting back up and staying in the game.

Pop's father was originally from Austria, the mountains near Yugoslavia. I think it was called Wiendish, but maybe not. His mom was from Trieste, which was an Italian city that had been won in some war by the Austrian-Hungarian empire.

Trieste became important as the only real seaport for that giant empire.

But then it became part of Italy again, a country with many great ports and harbors, so Trieste became an unimportant, peripheral jewel, with an opera house, boulevards, nice restaurants, and other special things left over from its royal glory days.

I went there once to visit Uncle Bruno and Aunt Marie. I was 19 years old, on leave from the Marine Corps, seeing some of northern Italy, including Venice and a visit to Uncle Bruno. It was lovely.

They lived in a big old apartment, had a boarder, a beautiful dark-haired girl, in her twenties. Bruno was semi-retired, making extra money writing sheet music by hand in the local music shop.

I was with them about five days. It was a nice visit, almost a time warp, like an impressionist painting, including the time I walked into the apartment and into the kitchen to find the boarder girl—we'll call her Gabriella, though I don't remember her name—standing in a large, galvanized tub, bathing. Her lovely back, long dark hair, and all. Old Aunt Marie on the other side, helping her bathe, a copper pot of warm water in her hand. With a shout and a gesture, Aunt Marie told me to get out, and scolded me later for intruding, like I should have known.

Gabriella never lost her poise in those few moments of perfect accident.

During the First World War, the brothers took different sides. Bruno, the eldest and most conservative, was a monarchist, and joined the Austrian Army. He was a musician, so became a courier-messenger, which is what bandsmen do at the front. Even now, even in the Marine Corps, they are the messengers.

Fighting the Russians, he was given a message to deliver. He told the Lieutenant: If you make me do this, I won't make it. I don't have a prayer.

He was told to go anyway and got picked off by the Russians. Shot in the ass, was so close to death that a Russian patrol found him and didn't even bother to finish him off.

Finally, days later, he was found by his own men, sent to Vienna to recover, and spent the rest of the war there as Regimental Band leader. A cushy job in a time of misery and privation. He even moved his mother-in law in with his wife and himself so they could feed and provide for her. Worked out well for his wife and her mother, but by war's end, it had wrecked Bruno's marriage.

In the Second World War, Bruno was a steward on an Italian merchant ship. A British warship captured them, and he spent the next four years on a prison farm in Kenya and became an expert farmer. No fences, no barbed wire, no locks, middle of Africa, nowhere to go.

When I asked about escaping, he smiled and said, no one even tried to penetrate the impenetrable.

Elysé, on the other hand, was a freethinker, and Pop's closest brother. He joined the French Army and survived. I don't know much about him, never got to meet him as he was killed later (before WWll) by Mussolini's Blackshirts at the printing shop where he and Pop published a communist newsletter.

His death broke something in Pop who was away from the shop at the time. He never talked much about Elysé.

Valerio was an artist. Impoverished and had consumption. The Army didn't want him. Pop said he was the sweetest of a tough bunch of kids. A gentle person, and another idealist. He is said to have died in a sanitarium in Venice.

Consumption got a lot of folks at that time. Pop made us crazy about it growing up. "Consumption, you'll get consumption!" Always checking to see if there were signs: shadows under our eyes or a lack of energy. I had no idea what he was raving about, but it was oppressive as hell. Later I found out it was tuberculosis, which we never had contact with in our generation.

When they came looking for Pop in The Great War (WWI), he ran off and hid in the hills. He was going to join up like everyone else, but a close friend came home from the front and the trenches—and, after seeing him, he changed his mind. His friend had been the biggest and strongest of their group. Robust, eager, full of confidence. He came home a skeleton, hunched over and morbidly depressed. His uniform hung on him like rags, he was almost unrecognizable. And most telling, he was terribly grateful just to be alive and not shot to pieces.

After that Pop decided he wasn't going to participate in their Great War. He was already reading Karl Marx and getting pumped up about Communism and how it would change things for a better world.

After the war, Pop started going to sea as a merchant marine. The Mediterranean for the most part, at that time. He crossed into Russia, through Turkey a number of times, and lived in Istanbul for a spell.

On one trip he made friends with a little Russian Jew who had been doing undercover work in Italy. He was heading back to Russia. Pop said, the little guy would never make it, he was a klutz.

Because of the revolution in Russia and the fear countries had of it, the border between Turkey and Russia was sealed and guarded.

Everyone the Turks caught sneaking back and forth, they beheaded the next day. Immigration solutions.

So Pop guided the little Jew across and took him all the way to Kiev. Pop had a Russian expat girlfriend in Istanbul and spoke some Russian. Anyway, the little guy was important, and a government official gave Pop an official thank you. In fact, they sometimes hired him as a sort of Russian/Turkish border coyote.

Concerning the Revolution, eventually his idealism waned. He said during the Czar, the rich aristocrats had bread and the poor didn't. After the Czar, the politicians had bread and the poor didn't. But once during the 1960s when I was protesting the Vietnamese war, he said to me, "You call that protesting? During the Revolution we protested with bullets, not cardboard signs!"

What to say?

But back then, Pop said he made a lot of money smuggling valuables and people out of Russia. So much so, he sent it back to Bruno to safe-keep for him. When he went back home to get the money, after a couple years, Bruno had spent it to furnish his house with new furniture. He said, "I was so sure you'd get killed, I never expected to see you again."

Over fifty years later Pop still hadn't warmed up much to Bruno.

Funny how it goes with people. Uncle Bruno came to America once, before the First War. Probably on a merchant ship. He stayed only a short while. He found it too raw, too wild, too crude, and went back to Vienna. Like I said, he was a Monarchist.

Pop on the other hand came with intentions to stay only a short while and then continue on to the Far East. But he loved it here, always loved it, and never left. Stayed, and made trouble.

Let me tell you a good story about Greenhorns and such. Pop lived in Brooklyn, where a lot of his fellow immigrants lived. (*Greenhorns* was the slang name for these European immigrants that were flooding into NYC. I don't know why they were called that, but I'm sure you can find out if you care to.)

He had a good friend in Brooklyn named Jerome (this was later, during the Depression.) Jerome lived with his mom in her big house. It had three apartments, and it was being foreclosed on by the bank. The whole country was full of homes being lost back to the banks, which did not want them back, but no one had money. Except a few who did, and Pop was one of them. Not so much, but some savings as he was a chef, and single, and had some luck in gambling.

Jerome was upset, losing their home, and his mom was beside herself. Pop said, "Look Jerome, let's let them foreclose; then we'll go to the bank auction and buy it back. They have more houses than they know what to do with and no one is buying."

So they went and they did. Pop fronted the cash. Bought the house back, free and clear, for $800 ... which Jerome would repay a little at a time. The Mom didn't even have to move out, but she did have to take the smaller apartment so they could rent her bigger one to stay afloat.

And the old woman never forgave Pop or her son Jerome for stealing her house.

As a young man, Pop spent some years in the Merchant Marines. He started out as a "coal-passer," i.e., carrying big shovels of coal from the boiler room coal storage to feed the giant steam boilers that powered the ship. Donato was a little bantam of a guy, about five foot five, and 150 lbs. Wiry and indomitable, but this work, deep in the hot bowels of the ship, near finished him.

Eventually he moved out of the pit, into the kitchen, and learned the art of being a pastry cook. Later in life, in the States he became a pastry chef, then a main course chef.

On this ship though, he was one of the many grunt seamen from all over that part of the world. One afternoon, he went to his bunk in the boiler-room crew's compartment to find his blanket missing.

That was unusual. It wasn't done on a ship at sea. He went looking for it and found it in another compartment, on someone else's bunk. That someone was a large, tall, very black African deckhand.

If you've seen black men from central Africa, you know they look very different from black men in the US, and their skin color is an almost surreal blue black.

Anyway, Donato told the deck hand that was his blanket and he was taking it back. The big man said something about that not happening. It was right about then that the African guy saw the glint of the straight razor opened in Pop's right hand. He told Pop to take his fricken blanket, if it meant that much, he didn't want it.

In my world, people don't use straight razors. I've been stabbed in a fight, but that was between a brick in my hand and a switch-blade. No one considered a razor. It's too cold, too visual—and with a straight razor, you have to do all the work yourself. Pop could. He had the right mix of heat and ice in his veins.

In 1958, my folks bought a small two-family on Campbell Ave, in Long Branch, New Jersey. A better part of town. It was the year I left home, joined the Marine Corps. Every time I came back home to visit for the next few years, Pop had modified the two apartments. To make them more presentable, he said. He kind of diced them up, added doorways, shifted walls, and made them pretty weird in my opinion.

Poor Mom was not happy with it, but couldn't say much.

One of the resulting oddities was that you could no longer reach the attic from the second floor. Pop sealed it off as if it never existed. Of course, there were windows at either end of the attic's peaked roof, so we knew it was still up there ... somewhere.

Lining the stairs going down to the basement was wainscoting. During one visit, Pop took me down there, and finding a barely noticeable separation in the wainscot, he pulled opened a hidden door.

He was full of surprises, almost always in ways you never saw coming.

Inside the hidden door was a dark narrow passageway going up into the house. On the floor was an extension cord, which Pop plugged into a nearby outlet. Way up top, a naked light bulb and socket hanging from a nail, lit up. In the dim light I saw an old home-made ladder reaching upward. It was aged but strong enough, though it did not inspire much confidence.

Pop led the way, and I followed him up to a small landing on the second-floor level. He then went through a rough hole broken into the wall, like a ship's small compartment door. You had to squeeze and hunch yourself to get through. Once through, in the dim light from the bulb, you found yourself in the shambles of what was once a second-floor washroom. I can still see the old green porcelain toilet, and a small cast-iron sink. Nothing was working, but it was all still hooked up, though shut off. A doorway exited the washroom into another small open area, with a flashlight lying on the floor.

Pop picked it up and turned it on to reveal another old wooden stepladder, a tall one, reaching up into the dimness. Up he went, slow but nimble, the ladder creaking. I, in serious amazement, trying not to get snagged on splinters of wood and old nails, followed our leader through these subterranean passageways, which terminated, as you can guess, in the attic.

Here we were, having tunneled up three floors, into the vanished attic. Its shades were dried out, cracking, and drawn. A few pieces of old furniture and a couple of wooden doors were stored in it. And it was layered in dust, except the center part where activity took place.

In so many words, but not directly, Pop let me know that this would be the family refuge for us kids and mom, and our kids when the "Blackshirts" came to round us up. Pop would not be with us, having led them on a fruitless chase to catch him. See, we'd have everything we needed, including the hidden bathroom that could be easily put in working order.

Mom? Yes, she had made the same trip I did. A small, plump woman in a powder blue housedress, scared of heights, and spiders, and always concerned about what Pop would come up with next. She said, through clenched teeth, that she had gone all the way up—like climbing Everest without a rope—and could not wait to get out of there.

Unfortunately, going back down was even more frightening, and she froze up at the top of the ladder. The fire department was not an option, who knows who's a Blackshirt? Seems like Pop had to keep his cool, be kind and gentle, and talk Mom out of there, a half a step at a time. And it took a while.

"Wow, Mom," I said, "that is something. What a project, but he did it." And of course, we couldn't tell anyone, because ....

Mom named it *The Mole Penthouse*. Referred to it as that but always with a sense of "... can you believe such a thing?" Being a Jew from Brooklyn, second generation, she did not have the same sense of urgency as Pop. Told me quietly, she wasn't sure whom we would be hiding from—but they'd have to just take her and put her on trial before she'd make that journey between the walls again.

I could tell Pop took pride and some reassurance for what he'd done for the family.

I kept the Mole Penthouse intact for many years, even after Pop had passed away. Like some memorable piece of heritage that you see sported here and there. A bunker from D-Day, a shelter from the blitz, a camp along the Oregon trail, Arthur Miller's writing desk.

Occasionally, I'd open the wainscoted hidden door, look inside, even go all the way up once in a while. And in the dust and half light, the ghosts of Karl Marx, and countless idealists, armed, in love, and now gone west, floated by ....

A cafeteria in Brooklyn, Greenhorns remaking the world over coffee—a safer world than the one they tried to remake in a Moscow cafeteria, drinking tea from giant samovars, making their rationed two lumps of sugar last the afternoon. Pop said he dropped his whole two lumps into *one* cup of tea, and the whole cafeteria stopped breathing. "Screw it, " he said, "at least I got one decent cup of tea that day."

At some point, not too long ago, I renovated the house, even made the attic into a light airy guest space, with easy access from the second floor.

Pop's homemade ladder—the one Mom climbed to the top of—hangs on the wall inside the storage shed in our backyard, next to an old kid's sled.

The wainscoted wall, the secret door, sealed shut, are still there. Sometimes, going past, I stop what I'm doing and stand quietly on the cellar stairs.

About the Author

Gary Galsworth was born and grew up in the New York City area. He spent three years in the Marine Corps before attending the Art Institute of Chicago and University of Chicago, majoring in painting and, later, in film making. He made a number of 16mm films during the late 1960s and 70s.

Along the way he learned the plumbing trade, initially to support his film work (*I couldn't drive my cab one more night*). He worked with Philip Glass and other artist-plumbers in that hotbed of creativity of the time, New York City.

Eventually he became a master plumber, moved to Hoboken, New Jersey with his family and started a plumbing business. "It was very hard but necessary. Business and plumbing made me get real about day-to-day life. Before that experience, I was in dreamland. It taught me to show up for the day I was actually in."

Gary became a student of Zen Practice in the 70s and has continued on this path of practice, complimented by Vipassana Meditation.

Poetry began as a quiet aside. One of his oldest poems, "Winter's Passing," is from 1964. The Mole Penthouse is his fourth book of poems. His three other collections are titled *Yes Yes*, *Beyond the Wire*, and *Nothing Itself*. All of them are available on Amazon.

His poetry has been featured in many literary journals, including in *Contemporary Expressions*, *Litbreak Magazine*, *Nebo*, *Abstract*, *Pennsylvania English*, *Pioneertown*, *Poydras Review*, *Temenos*, *Broad River Review*, *Riverfeet Press*, *Main Street Rag*, and *Obsidian*.

Gary has two children, now grown—his daughter, Ondine, and his son, Daniel—both living in the NYC area.

Gary lives in Hoboken, New Jersey and Providence, Rhode Island, with his lovely wife, Carol, a nurse practitioner.

He can be reached at *gdplumber@aol.com*.

www.ingramcontent.com/pod-product-compliance
Lightning Source LLC
LaVergne TN
LVHW041249080426
835510LV00009B/664